THE VOYAGES OF CHRISTOPHER COLUMBUS

Random House, New York

THE VOYAGES OF

CHRISTOPHER COLUMBUS

Written and Illustrated by

ARMSTRONG SPERRY

CONTENTS

THE VOYAGES OF CHRISTOPHER COLUMBUS

CHAPTER 1

Refuge

"Courage, my son. are you very weary?"

"Yes, Father," the child answered. "Have we a long way still to go?"

The man pointed up the hill. There a massive building crouched like a watchdog above the seaport of Palos. Its painted walls were flushed with the afterglow of the sun. A sound of vesper bells drifted across the still air.

"We are almost arrived," the man said.

"Look! The monastery of Our Lady of La Rabida. For tonight, it is the end of our journey."

The little boy's fingers tightened on the man's. "And will we find rest there?" he demanded hopefully. "And food?"

"For certain," the man reassured him. "The good Franciscans never close the door to one who hungers."

But it was a steep climb up the hill. Long before the two travelers reached the monastery, the man was forced to carry his son. They had covered many miles since dawn. The dust of Spain lay like a powder on their boots and clothing. The day had been unbearably hot, even for that summer of 1491, and the heat had pulled at their muscles, drained their limbs of strength.

With a sigh of relief the man set the boy down upon the doorstep. Then he lifted the silver knocker and let it fall against the ancient worm-bored panel of the door. The noise of the summons echoed through the silence.

As he stood waiting, the man cast a backward glance down the hill whence he and his small son had come. Across the vineyards and beyond the tiled rooftops of Palos, the masts of many ships could be seen on the darkening waters of the Rio Tinto.

Beyond the bar of Saltes, a magnificent galleon was standing out to the open sea. Her sails were dyed blood-red by the Andalusian sun, her flags and pennants whipping on the wind. The man's heart quickened. What would he not have given for such a ship! She was on a westward tack, but her captain would change that soon enough. Men didn't sail into the Sea of Darkness that lay at the western edge of the earth! They sailed south to Guinea, or east to the Golden Horn, or sometimes north as far as Iceland; but never into the unknown West.

"Fools!" the man muttered. "Why won't they listen to me?"

There came a sound of sandals flapping on a tiled floor. Then the monastery door swung heavily. A stout little monk, dressed in the humble gown and hood of his order, stared with short-sighted eyes at the two strangers on the doorstep. Though their clothing was shabby, they had not the look of beggars.

"And what might you be seeking?" the monk queried.

"Of your charity, Brother, we seek shelter for the night," the man replied wearily. "A loaf to eat; a cup of milk perhaps——"

The little monk's eyes twinkled. The coming of a stranger, especially one who spoke with a foreign accent, was an event. "There is enough for two and to spare," he said eagerly. "The bread is fresh-baked and the goats have just been milked."

"You are kind to a stranger," the weary traveler said.

"Tsk! It is nothing." The monk smiled. "You have come far?"

"Aye. From Portugal."

"Tsk! Tsk!" The good brother clucked with amazement. "Many days of travel! You must indeed be weary. You are a Portuguese, then?"

"I am an Italian, of Genoa," the stranger replied.

"Indeed!" the brother exclaimed. "And to what name do you answer?"

Unconsciously the man on the doorstep stiffened to full height, and the monk saw that though he was of middle age, he was spare and strongly built. His brow was lofty, his chin squared off, and his nose was as bold as the prow of a ship. Gravely the stranger answered: "Men call me Christopher Columbus. This lad is my son, Diego."

The monk beamed upon them. "I am known as Brother Sebastian," he confided. "Enter, my friends, and be at peace. Our Prior is at the moment engaged but he will receive you shortly."

Now, the Franciscan lay-brother has ever been as noted for his love of talk as for his hospitality. Brother Sebastian proved no exception. Maintaining a running fire of question and comment, he led the two travelers down a dim corridor, then through a courtyard where pomegranates and fig trees stood motionless in the dusk.

It was good to hear news, he said. How stood matters in Portugal? How fared the King? Did Columbus know that here in Spain, King Ferdinand and Queen Isabella were engaged in a death-struggle to drive the Moors forever from this gracious land?

Quite out of breath, Brother Sebastian flung open a pair of doors. "Take your ease here in the library," he invited, "while I see to the supper.

Then I shall inform the Prior that you are here. You will find Father Perez a most wise and learned man. His mind is as full of knowledge as a nut is full of meat. And let me tell you, he is a man of no ordinary connections! Once he was father-confessor to the noble Queen Isabella herself."

With which, the little monk bustled away, leaving a wake of silence. Gratefully the small boy sank into a chair, exhausted; but his father glanced about the library with quickening interest. Row upon row of books, richly bound in fine leathers, lined the walls of the lofty room. A long table was strewn with scrolls and maps. On a work-bench stood an unfinished model of a caravel; and Columbus's practiced eye noted the exact detail with which the little ship was being made. Surely the Prior, or one of the lay-brothers, must have an uncommon interest in ships and the sea.

An astrolabe—an instrument used in astronomy—drew the man's attention. He moved toward it as if drawn by some force within the metal itself. Slowly he reached out and touched it. With that contact it seemed as if the library

with its walls of books receded from him, van-
ishing completely.

Once again his spirit went leaping into the
dark toward some star invisible to all but him.
How they had laughed at him in Portugal! They
called him a dreamer, an addle-pate, an impostor. And the great King John had laughed loud-
est of all. "I suppose, O most wise Columbus,"
he had said, "that on the other side of this globe
you speak of, men walk upside down and trees
grow with their branches hanging downward.
And there it rains and snows and hails *upward*!
Is this so?" The Court had rocked with laughter.

The man's fists knotted. For a second he shut
his eyes to the memory of those hateful faces,
Closed his ears to the echo of their mocking
laughter.

Suddenly he felt a tugging at his sleeve.
"Father," Diego pleaded. "Brother Sebastian
brings our supper. Let us eat! I am starved."

The man's hand dropped on the child's head.
His eyes were bitter as he thought: "My poor
motherless boy. What is to become of you in this
world of blind men and fools, where even the
most learned see no farther than the end of their

noses?" Aloud, he said: "Yes, my son, let us eat."

The tray which Brother Sebastian placed upon the table offered a loaf of bread still warm from the oven; a jug of goat's milk; a plate of cold meats; a bowl of oranges.

"This should fortify you till the morrow," said the little monk, smiling. He lighted tapers at each end of the table, and his eyes danced as he watched the man and the boy address themselves to the food spread before them. They ate in utter silence, as if famished, causing the good brother to restrain his desire to talk. Later, brother Sebastian would learn all about this stranger with the burning eyes and the lines of bitterness carved about his mouth. Surely this was no ordinary traveler! What misadventures could have brought this man called Christopher Columbus, with a child in his arms, to the doors of Our Lady of La Rabida?

With the last mouthful of food, little Diego's head nodded. Manfully he struggled against the weight of his eyelids; but his thin body slumped forward. One cheek rested on the table.

"He sleeps," murmured Brother Sebastian.

"He is small for such a journey, Señor Columbus. I shall carry him to his bed. Father Perez will join you here shortly. He has been told that you are waiting." The monk stooped and gently lifted the sleeping child.

After the good brother's departure, the room seemed filled with shadow. Through the open window drifted the voices of the Franciscans singing the Compline: the last service of the day. The tapers burned steadily in the motionless air.

Columbus sat quite still, lost in brooding. Had he been unwise to flee to Spain? True, there had been no choice in the matter, for only here could he take ship to France. The Portuguese had denied him the right to leave their country. They had stolen his maps and calculations and sent out ships secretly. Yet God had punished them, for their ships had been blown back on their own coasts.

But Columbus had been forced to slink like a thief across the frontier, dragging the child with him. Would he be any more successful in persuading the King of France that the shortest route to the fabled wealth of the Far East lay by sailing *west*?

Suddenly Columbus smote the table with the flat of his hand. He must, he *would* convince the French king! There wasn't so much time any more. The years were slipping away like birds in a mist. Would he live long enough to bring to reality this dream he saw so clearly? Why could he not make others see that dream, too? It seemed that men thought of the oceans only as boundaries beyond which lay destruction. But there were no boundaries to the human spirit.

The man's head sank into his hands. His body stilled. And as he slept, his mind went drifting backward to another place, to a time when he was young again, and the sky was bluer than any sky he remembered since childhood. Whose voice was that calling to him? Ah, now he remembered! It was Bartolomeo, his older brother, crying: "Let's go down to the wharf! There's a ship in from Guinea, with sailors who wear rings of gold in their ears. Come, let's go!"

"Aye!" Christopher shouted back eagerly; for what could be more fun than to see a ship from Guinea, whose sailors wore rings of gold in their ears?

"Aye, Bartolomeo, let's go!"

CHAPTER 2

The Prior of
La Rabida

HOW COULD THE TWO BOYS HAVE GUESSED
that aboard that ship would be their sailor-
cousin, Tonio, gone from Genoa these many
months? They met him on a narrow strip of
beach. A big oafish fellow, dull of wit, Tonio was
now cloaked in the glory of one who has voyaged
to mysterious lands. But Christopher hung back.
He had never liked Tonio.

[15]

It was Bartolomeo who demanded eagerly: "Tell us, cousin, where have you been all these months? Did you see the Grand Khan, or the Emperor of Cipango?"

"I've been to the sandy beaches of Barbary, my little stay-at-homes," Tonio answered loftily. "I've seen the Pillars of Hercules, and those new islands discovered by the Portuguese——"

"You mean the Fortunate Isles?" Christopher asked, speaking up.

Tonio swung toward the boy. His eyes rounded with astonishment. "So you've heard of them! I remember you were always with your nose in a book. You'll be a monk one day if you don't watch out. Have the books told you that at Antioch, beyond Greece, the sea comes to an end?"

"I don't believe it," Christopher scoffed. "Fishermen's tales!"

"*Holá!*" the other retorted, nettled. "You know more than the mariners, perhaps?"

"I know," the boy answered stubbornly, "that Father Giovanni read us a book in the Weavers' School—written by a man of Venice. His name was Marco Polo. *He* said——"

But Tonio interrupted rudely. "I've heard of that one! A giant of a liar."

"Indeed he's not!" Christopher warmed with anger. "Everything in that book is just as Marco Polo saw it. Father Giovanni says so. He was Viceroy to the Grand Khan for many years. He rode on white elephants whose tusks were banded with gold, and who wore bracelets of silver bells on their ankles. He traveled far beyond the country of the Khan, beyond Cathay— as far as the island of Cipango. He said the very roofs of the houses were made of gold and studded with precious stones. I shall go there myself one day!"

Tonio gave a great laugh and slapped his thigh. "But our small rooster makes a large noise," he bellowed. "And what else do you plan to do, Wise One?"

The boy's lips set in a firm line, and in his eyes there blazed a sudden purpose. "One day I shall own my own caravel," he said proudly. "And I shall sail through the Pillars of Hercules, down the Barbary Coast, always to the west . . ."

"To the *west?*" echoed Tonio, blinking. "Are

you daft, rooster? No mariner dares to enter those waters. The waves there roll high as mountains. And the sea is full of huge monsters that can swallow a ship, sails and all."

It was Christopher's turn to be scornful. "How do you know?" he demanded. "If anyone ever met with such monsters, how could he return to tell about them?"

Tonio's slow wits were no match for his young cousin's. His face took on the dark and sullen look that the boy remembered so well.

"You see," Bartolomeo put in, uneasily, "our Christopher believes that the earth is a globe, that there's no beginning or end to it."

"Of course it's a globe," Christopher insisted. "When you look out to sea, have you never noticed that the topmasts of a ship are visible long before you see the ship itself? When you travel on land, haven't you observed that it's the peaks of the mountains you see first? How could this be so if the earth were flat?"

Tonio shifted uncomfortably.

"Look here!" cried Christopher. From his pocket he drew a dark stone that he had picked up on the beach weeks before. It was almost completely round. On its smooth surface the boy had scratched with flint a series of lines and curves. "Let me show you——" and now his voice was earnest. "Father Giovanni has helped me with this. These long lines are the Mediterranean Sea. Genoa is right *here*. Eastward, across Asia, the road runs to Cathay and Cipango. Those lands are the eastern end of the inhabited world. Beyond that, there's nothing but water. Here in the west you see the coast of Africa, Portugal and Spain."

The boy twirled the round stone under the astonished eyes of his audience. Bartolomeo was speechless with admiration for his clever brother. But Tonio's face was dark with disbelief.

"At the top of the globe," Christopher hurried on, "it's always icy-cold. The sea is white as goat's milk and the air is thick with mist. The people there clothe themselves in the hides of animals. I shall never go there! But here in the west, the earth doesn't come to an end with Africa and Spain. The Portuguese have already discovered a whole new archipelago lying in front of Cape Verde." He gripped the stone tighter and suddenly his young voice deepened.

"This is how I shall sail to the Indies in my caravel——From Genoa I'll sail straight through the Pillars of Hercules, on toward the west. Farther and farther on the open ocean. And at last I shall come to the lands of the East—the kingdom of the Grand Khan. Men will never need camels again. Only ships, ships, ships!" His eyes were shining like stars.

But Tonio made a sound of rage. "Liar!" he shouted thickly. "Watch your tongue, boy!" With the flat of his palm he struck Christopher a terrible blow.

The boy staggered, fell headlong to the sand. The round stone rolled into the sea.

Columbus lifted his head. Where was he? What had happened? Where were Bartolomeo and Tonio? All around him was darkness through which he could not see. Suddenly then a light appeared before his eyes as a taper flared. Above the taper a grave elderly face, framed in a monk's cowl, looked steadily into his own.

"You have slept, Señor Columbus," a deep rich voice was saying. "I found you in darkness.

The tapers had burned out. You were lost in dreams."

"Who—are you?" Columbus stammered, half rising.

"I am Father Perez," the man answered quietly. "Prior of Our Lady of La Rabida. I bid you welcome, señor."

"Your kindness embarrasses me, Father," the other managed.

"Brother Sebastian has already told me your name and that you come from Portugal. But I do not know your way of life." The Prior remained standing, as if undecided whether to encourage this stranger or put a speedy end to his visit.

"I am a mariner, Father, and a maker of maps," Columbus answered.

At once Father Perez took seat on the opposite side of the table. His interest had been immediately caught; for the learned Prior of La Rabida had long been a student of astronomy and geography. "So!" he echoed, "A maker of maps. I myself have given much thought to the mysteries of the heavens and the earth." As he spoke, he smiled and laid a hand lovingly on the model of the caravel which Columbus previously had noted. "But now and again I play a little," he confessed. "This ship-model is one of my playthings. Tell me—as a mariner you have voyaged far?" There was a hint of eagerness in the grave voice, a glimmer of youthful light in the dark eyes. This elderly man, garbed in the sober habit of Saint Francis, spoke of ships and the sea as only one could who yearned for them.

Columbus warmed to his host. For so long he had been treated with ridicule that now he expanded in the glow of the Prior's interest. "For thirty years, as man and boy, I have followed the sea," he said. "I have crossed the Mediterranean times without number and touched all its coasts. I have been to the English islands, to the Portuguese Azores, to Iceland, and to the Spanish archipelago of the Canaries."

For a second, doubt flickered in the Prior's eyes. "That means you have touched the very boundaries of the whole world, señor."

"Of the known world, yes," Columbus replied. "But not of the whole world. I believe there are still other lands, perhaps continents, to be discovered."

"Indeed! How can you state that so surely, since you have never seen them?"

A sudden smile robbed Columbus's answer of its edge. "How can you state that there is a Heaven, Father, since you have never seen it?"

"Because I believe in it," the Prior answered quietly.

"Exactly! And I share that belief. But to it I add—mathematics."

Father Perez nodded his head thoughtfully. "It is possible," he admitted. "After all, the Canaries were only discovered in my father's time."

From within his shabby doublet, Columbus drew a folded parchment carefully wrapped in waxed silk. He spread it on the table.

"Look you, Father," he explained, eagerly. "The only chart the Portuguese didn't get away from me! It is a map I have drawn of those unknown regions. Although I have not seen them, I know from the facts we already have what those far-off lands must be like."

"Of what facts do you speak?" And Father Perez' tone was cautious. This stranger, he felt uneasily, might be either a lunatic or a genius.

Columbus warmed to his subject. "Gales blowing from the west have washed ashore on Porto Santo timbers of unknown wood, carved without the touch of iron!" he exclaimed. "What hand carved them? And bamboos, too, so thick that one section could hold gallons of wine; and trees, the like of which do not grow in the Azores. Whence did they come? The Governor of Flores himself reported the bodies of two men cast up by the ocean—men with yellow faces and straight black hair, like the people of Asia. What of all this?"

For a second the Prior was silent, touched by a sense of wonder and of awe. Hesitantly, he said: "But who could be found to face such monstrous perils on an unknown ocean? The very thought is terrifying."

A rare smile lighted Columbus's somber face. "He who would make sure of dying in bed should never go to sea," he answered. Suddenly he picked an orange from the bowl on the table. "Consider for a moment, Father, that this is the world," he pleaded. "This point we shall call Lisbon. And here—" he marked another point on the fruit, "is the uttermost region of

Cathay: a distance of fourteen thousand miles. Now, instead of voyaging east by land, suppose we sail west by water. What will happen? We shall reach Cathay by traveling only four thousand miles. Think of it! Four thousand miles by sea rather than fourteen thousand by land."

A wry smile twisted the Prior's lips. "You have, it seems, an answer to all objections. But tell me—to what good end do you desire to prove your theory?"

Proudly Columbus's answer came back: "To find the shortest route to the continent of Asia, and to bring to its people a knowledge of the true Faith." There was no mistaking the ringing sincerity of the words. "I believe, good Father, that God has called me to this mission—in giving me, since childhood, a love of far places. He has taught me the secrets of the stars and the sea. He has granted me wisdom for mathematics and skill for making charts. Until I cease to breathe, I must follow His bidding."

The man broke off, made a gesture of helplessness. "And what do I ask for this great venture? Only three ships. Three small ships. Is that so much to ask?"

The Prior sank his chin in thought while the tapers burned low. In his mind the belief was growing that this man called Christopher Columbus, this stranger who had chanced to knock at the doors of La Rabida, had pierced to the heart of the truth.

Conscious now of a great fatigue, Columbus arose and pushed back his chair. That sense of failure which had weighed upon him so heavily and so long had returned. "I have taxed your kindness unduly, Father," he said in a low tone; and folding the chart, replaced it in his doublet. "If you will show me to the chamber where my child sleeps——The hour is late and we must be off at dawn."

"Off?" The Prior roused himself. "To where?"

"I seek a ship to France. To offer this empire of which I speak, this great glory, to the French King."

"But——"

"I have lost too many years already!" the man cried bitterly. "Fourteen of them I gave to Portugal. And for what? They stole my calculations, promising to study them and give me a decision. But secretly they sent out the ships they refused to give me. Now their fleets creep along the coasts of Guinea, getting here a bit of gold and there a Negro slave. But I shall secure for the French Crown a direct route across the western ocean to the vast wealth of Asia."

"But why for the French King?" the Prior objected. "Why not for King Ferdinand and Queen Isabella, when already you stand on the soil of Spain?"

"There is no sovereign I would more gladly serve than Isabella of Castile," said Columbus heavily. "But how should I ever command the ear of Her Majesty?"

"It is not beyond possibility," the Prior answered slowly, "though this is scarcely the moment to petition Their Majesties for ships and funds. The war with the Moors has drained the Treasury. Still, a thought presents itself to me——"

"And that, good Father?"

"It occurs to me that this port of Palos is under sentence of the Royal Council to furnish two ships for any service the Crown may appoint. With two provided, the cost of a third ship might not seem so formidable to the Queen."

Such a hope surged in Columbus's breast that he could not trust himself to speak; for he remembered that the Prior had once been father-confessor to Queen Isabella herself.

Father Perez was saying: "I shall show you now to your chamber. We will sleep on the notion. Sleep brings wise counsel." And then for a second his thin old body stiffened. He stared into the other's eyes, probing deep. What he discovered must have satisfied him, for he said: "It takes courage to be the first to do a thing which the world needs. The little men turn back and the cowards never start. In me you have found a friend. I believe in you, Christopher Columbus. And remember that the longest day, however hard, has an evening; the longest journey, an end. Go with God, señor."

Columbus bowed his head. Tears stood in his eyes. "God bless and keep you, Father," he whispered.

CHAPTER 3

A Cause Sponsored

THE LAWS OF SPAIN THAT SUMMER OF 1491
strictly informed a shipmaster which ports he
might touch and what goods he could carry. But
the seamen of Palos, ever an independent breed,
had frequently broken the law by dealing in
forbidden goods. This defiance of the Crown
finally exhausted the patience of the Royal
Council. The penalty was severe. The parish of
Palos was ordered to equip two ships at the ex-

pense of its inhabitants, and hold them at the pleasure of the Crown. For a term of one year they could be dispatched on whatever service might be ordered.

This sentence caused much grumbling in the seaport. No man knew whose ships might be seized, which sailors pressed into service, or on what ill-omened journey they might be sent. After some weeks, however, of no further discipline, the people settled down to a belief that the Royal Council was only threatening them into better behavior.

They would have been astonished to learn that in the mind of the Prior of La Rabida, an idea was forming which would unsettle their feeling that all was well.

During the hours immediately following his interview with Christopher Columbus, the worthy father tossed restlessly on his hard bed. Through his wakeful thoughts the rooftops of Cipango gleamed like purest gold. The treasures of Cathay—jewels and precious metals and spices and silks—would fill to overflowing the royal coffers which had been drained by war. Too, Father Perez thought of the millions of people in heathen Asia who might be brought into the Faith. It was unthinkable that such an empire, such an opportunity, should be lost to Spain!

Small wonder that Father Perez tossed on his pallet, while doubts and uncertainties plagued him. Though for many years he had been father-confessor to the Queen, he never had taken advantage of her favor. Would he be right in so doing this once? Could he have been mistaken in his judgment of this map-maker, this Genoese whose eyes blazed with a such a lofty purpose?

By dawn the sleepless Prior was determined to seek the help of others in confirming his own belief. Who better could advise him than Garcia Fernandez, physician to the town? This worthy doctor's knowledge was broad and his studies extended far beyond the limits of medicine. His familiarity with astronomy and geography was as sound as the Prior's own. Too, there was Martin Alonzo Pinzon, wealthy merchant and ship-owner. Pinzon came of an old seafaring family and himself was a mariner of experience.

To his practical knowledge of navigation, he brought a thoughtful mind and much common sense.

"Yes," stated Father Perez half aloud, "these are the very men whose judgment must confirm my own."

Thus, no sooner were the morning services in the chapel over, and a simple meal eaten, than the Prior sent Brother Sebastian into the town with a message. The immediate presence of Garcia Fernandez and Martin Pinzon was requested in the library of La Rabida. The matter, it was stated, was urgent.

Before the hour of noon, Christopher Columbus found himself faced with the problem of winning over these two influential men. A night's sleep had refreshed him. While young Diego worked in the garden with Brother Sebastian, Columbus spoke of his plans with a clear mind and a high heart. Matters were moving fast now. After so many years of discouragement it was difficult to believe in his sudden good fortune. Surely he could persuade these two men to have faith in his enterprise, as already he had persuaded the wise Prior.

But it would not be easy. He found Fernandez a severe, even formidable-looking man, whose bony framework seemed to show through the black gabardine that clothed it. But under the black skull-cap that crowned his high-domed forehead, the doctor's eyes were fine and intelligent. In their clear cool depths Columbus read encouragement. But this was not a man to be easily swayed.

Martin Pinzon was cast in a different mold. This man who was to play so important a part in Columbus's life was square-built and powerful. Above the middle height, he was dressed as befitted a wealthy merchant, in a surcoat of dark-red velvet trimmed with fur. His hose were of silk, his boots of finest Cordovan leather. Handsome rings flashed on his fingers. But his blue eyes had the far-sighted gaze of the sailor and his manner, too, was forthright and hearty. Both of these men had given much thought to the very theories Columbus now expounded, and Pinzon had navigated much of the known world.

The respectful attention of such an audience fanned the glow of Columbus's ardor. Never had he stood in such need of the right words;

never had they come more readily to his command. And such was the moving power of his speech that even before he came to the consideration of his chart and calculations, he felt that both these men had been fired by his dream. Father Perez, watching silently, saw the shadow of doubt fade from the eyes of Garcia Fernandez. There was no mistaking the hearty enthusiasm of Martin Pinzon.

When Columbus produced his chart, the two men bent with absorbed interest above it, even as the Prior had done the night before. Out of their separate knowledge, Fernandez and Pinzon recognized the skill with which the map-maker had drawn the known world, and the daring vision that suggested a new one.

Springing to his feet, Pinzon let out a great cry. "By my faith! We would be unworthy to call ourselves Spaniards if we let such a discovery slip through our fingers." His face was alive with excitement. He began to pace the library as if it were the quarterdeck of a ship.

Thoughtfully, Garcia Fernandez fingered his beard. "Your plan is so sound, Señor Columbus,"

he said, "so near to what my own studies have
suggested! But I must confess, I do not own
your power of imagination."

Columbus was elated. "All I need is the ships,
doctor. Three ships—and, the men to sail them."

"What manner of vessel had you in mind for
such a voyage?" asked the practical Pinzon.

"The very same as are used along these
coasts," came the ready answer. "They are seaworthy, yet not too deep of draught to sail in
shallow waters, or to navigate a river."

Pinzon smote one fist into the palm of his
other hand. "A small consideration in view of
such an undertaking. It happens that, by God's
grace, I own more than enough of this world's
goods. Men call me wealthy and it is so. It
would be possible for me to underwrite your
voyage, Señor Columbus. State your needs,
sir——"

But Columbus shook his head in firm refusal.
"A voyage such as I propose calls for the authority of the Crown behind it," he said. "That is the
reason I have spent so many years knocking at
the door of kings. I shall be appointed Viceroy

to any lands I discover—a position that could be maintained only by the forces which a monarch could command."

"Spoken with wisdom," agreed Father Perez. "This is a matter beyond private enterprise."

"I am told," Garcia Fernandez put in," that the people of Palos are under compulsion to produce two ships for the service of the Crown."

"Quite so," smiled the Prior. "But our good townsmen must not be consulted beforehand. They are not eager to part with what they once hold."

"But," the other protested, "they must yield to a direct order from our Sovereigns. Do you think, Father, that such an order could be procured?"

Cautiously the Prior wagged his head. "This is an unfortunate moment to beg for royal favor. If the present siege fails, our good Sovereigns may never drive the Moors from this land. But——" And here Father Perez paused significantly. His audience stared at him. Columbus scarcely dared to breathe. "In all humility, I say that if anyone may command the ear of

our Lady Queen, it is I. With two ships accounted for, I shall endeavor to persuade her to find means to equip a third." Saying which, Father Perez picked up a silver bell and rang it violently.

From the direction of the garden Brother Sebastian came hurrying as fast as his years and stoutness would allow. Little Diego trailed at his heels.

"You rang, Father?" the monk panted, breathless.

"Make haste!" cried the Prior. "See that the mule, Teresa, is saddled at once."

The monk blinked. "Your Reverence goes on a journey——?"

"To Salamanca, to seek audience with our Queen."

Brother Sebastian gulped. "Your Reverence will forgive me, I do hope, for what I am about to say——"

"Speak up! Time presses."

"Salamanca is many leagues away, Father," stammered Brother Sebastian. "It is too far (my pardon) for one of your years."

"Heaven is even farther," snapped the Prior,

"yet I expect to go there one day. The mule, see to it at once." He turned to Columbus, grasped his hand warmly. "In the meantime, my friend, this poor retreat will consider itself fortunate if you use its shelter until we know the pleasure of the Queen."

Diego slipped his hand excitedly into his father's. "What does it mean, Father?" he whispered. "Tell me——"

Christopher Columbus looked down at his small son. The lines about his mouth softened. "It means, my Diego, that God at last has smiled upon me. I am the most fortunate of men."

After the Prior's departure, Columbus spent long hours in the library, poring over the rich collection of volumes. Now and again he would join Diego in the garden, where he worked with the younger monks. Already the boy had become a great favorite and delighted in making himself useful.

Thus the days passed. Two weeks slipped into a third. The month drew to a close. And then, late one afternoon, it was Diego who first discovered the mule, Teresa, with Father Perez enveloped in a cloud of dust, coming up the hill from Palos.

Excitement swept like a wind through the quiet of the monastery. With a haste unseemly to their order the monks flocked to greet their Prior. Columbus's heart beat high. Anxious though he was, he waited for Father Perez to speak.

"Thanks be to God!" cried the Prior, slipping off the mule's back. He swayed with fatigue. "But I am an old man and my years weigh heavily." His eye fell upon Columbus; his face glowed. "I have good word for you, my friend. Our Lady Queen enjoys the same noble heart as always."

"You mean, Father——?"

"Patience, my son. I must rest. Then we will converse."

Later, when he had been refreshed, the good father informed his audience of all that had taken place during his interview with Queen Isabella. "She has sent twenty thousand *maravedis** to defray the cost of your journey to Sala-

* About $216.00.

manca," he said happily, "and to buy yourself garments suitable for conferring with the great ones of Spain."

"Then I am to have audience with the Queen herself?" stammered Columbus, scarce daring to believe in his good fortune.

"Not so fast, my friend," the other warned. "She has given me letters to influential persons —to the royal treasurer, Don Luis de Santangel; to Hernando de Talavera, Bishop of Avila, and to the great Duke of Medina-Celi. Moreover, Her Majesty has appointed a court of fourteen learned men to listen to your case and pass judgment. In the event you win their approval, Isabella will give you audience and sponsor your undertaking."

These words dampened the high hopes of Columbus. Too often he had been thwarted by the stupidity of so-called learned men. "I had hoped for audience with the Queen herself, rather than her minions," he said gloomily.

"And so had I," answered the Prior. "But we must do with what we have. A sturdy mule is necessary for the journey. In Salamanca you will lodge with the tailor Bensabat, who will make you suitable clothing. And while you are gone, your son will be safe in my keeping. You are to have no thought except for your great undertaking."

But the peace which had been in Columbus's mind during these days of waiting for Father Perez to return, was now disturbed. In its place was a sense of uncertainty, as if he stood outside a locked door behind whose panels were mysteries he would not care to solve.

Quietly he said: "From my heart I thank you, Father, for all that you have done in my behalf."

"You must walk with caution, my son," the other warned. "There are men in Salamanca who will question your beliefs as heresy. If you should be unlucky enough to offend the Holy Office of the Inquisition, the Queen herself could not save you!"

Columbus's smile was rueful. "I shall try to walk with caution, though it is not my natural gait. Give me your blessing, good Father."

Kneeling like a dutiful son, he pressed to his lips the fine old hand of Father Perez.

CHAPTER 4

The Judgment

BENSABAT, THE TAILOR, LOOKED AT HIS LODGER with open admiration. This was a Christopher Columbus far different from the shabby stranger who, some weeks before, had begged refuge at the gates of La Rabida.

Never had Bensabat used his needle more effectively. Over a doublet of darkest olive velvet, with matching hose and a crisp ruff, Columbus wore a surcoat on which strange designs

were embroidered in thread-of-silver. The puffed
sleeves added inches to the natural width of his
shoulders. There was a flat velvet cap of the
same olive color, with a red plume clasped by a
silver buckle. Here, one would have said, stood
a man of affairs. Only the bronzed cheek and
mariner's gait bespoke long years at sea.

"What shall I do with your old clothing,
Señor Columbus?" Bensabat asked, chuckling.

"Give it to the first beggar who knocks."

The tailor reached into a pocket and produced
an envelope of finest parchment. It was fixed
with a heavy seal of gold wax and stamped with
a signet. "A servant of His Excellency Don Luis
de Santangel has just brought this message,
señor." And Bensabat added slyly: "It seems
that the new doublet has been finished not an
hour too soon! De Santangel is one of the great
names of the land."

Don Luis de Santangel, the Royal Treasurer
. . . Columbus's pulse leaped as he broke the
golden seal. For more than a week he had been
cooling his heels in this university city where,
upon orders from the Court, the learned doctors
would sit in judgment on his plan. Impatiently

his eye raced through the message. It informed him that the judges would receive him that very afternoon at the fourth hour in the fortress of Salamanca.

"You desire nothing else, señor?"

"Nothing. You may go, Bensabat."

After the tailor's departure, Columbus took to a nervous pacing, up and down, back and forth. The room seemed too narrow for his big frame. He felt ill at ease in his new finery. How he longed to feel once again a deck beneath his feet! He had been too long at anchor and now his body yearned for honest action.

But the gravity of the ordeal before him was sobering. De Santangel had already stated that of the fourteen judges who would hear him, ten were churchmen. "As well," Columbus had thought bitterly, "ask a friar how to navigate a ship!" But he was fully aware of the risk he took in running counter to the beliefs of the older clergy. For the Inquisition was in full force. Thousands of victims were being put to death for heresy. Men guarded their most secret thoughts, uncertain of friend or foe. They walked warily, fearful of tripping over their tongue. No one was safe, no one too innocent to be proved guilty. The Inquisition was a terrifying power greater than the King's.

How would Columbus fare? Would his plan be accorded an honest discussion? Or would he find himself face to face with a tribunal? Of one thing he was certain: he would have to stand firm. Whatever happened, he must not lose his nerve now. Surely he had not survived all these years of trial and frustration to perish as a heretic!

The lofty battlements of Salamanca towered against the sky. Cathedral bells tolled the first stroke of four as the figure in olive velvet hurried across an old Roman bridge.

At the outer gate of the fortress, the guard scanned the seal of de Santangel's missive, then let its bearer pass without challenge. At the inner gate a porter said: "The noble doctors are expecting you, Señor Columbus. For two hours already they have been debating."

Down a gloomy corridor the porter led the way, to halt at last before a pair of iron-studded doors. From the other side came a rumble of voices. Above that murmur of sound, one voice shrilled as if in anger. The doors opened. Columbus stepped through into a vaulted chamber of great height, filled with shadows.

A table shaped like a horseshoe confronted him. It was covered with red velvet and supplied with writing materials. He recognized his own map, the pages of his calculations; the fourteen men grouped around that table had been thumbing them through. Out of the murky light of candles emerged the white robes and black cloaks of the Dominicans, the brown fabric of the Franciscans; but most of the men's faces were shadowed by cowls. There were four others whose caps and gleaming chains of office proclaimed them doctors of the university.

For a moment no one remarked Columbus's presence, all attention being fixed upon the speaker with the rasping voice. Then someone caught Columbus by the arm, drew him down into an empty chair. It was Diego de Deza, Prior of the Dominicans.

"Silence!" he whispered. "Your turn to talk will come soon enough."

A sense of foreboding fixed itself upon Co-

Don Luis

lumbus as he listened to the speaker who was commanding such rapt attention. The man's eyes burned like embers in dark sockets. His nose was the beak of a hawk. In a voice that grated he cried out:

"And lastly—who *is* this starveling, this impostor? He is no son of Spain, no subject of our illustrious sovereigns. He is a foreigner of doubtful origin, a Genoese whose people were weavers. And from time out of mind Genoa has been the cradle of heresy!"

The speaker sat down abruptly, drawing his cowl about his head. Through the sudden silence rippled a murmur of assent. Columbus's heart chilled.

The Dominican Prior rose to his feet, held up one hand to ask for silence. "Señor Columbus is among us, gentleman," de Deza said. "He stands prepared to answer any question. Let those who have questions put them in due order."

From the center of the table came the thin sharp voice of Hernando de Talavera, Bishop of Avila. In those chiseled features Christopher Columbus could discover no hint of warmth or sympathy.

"We have given careful consideration to the chart and calculations submitted by Señor Columbus," the Bishop said, and a suggestion of mockery colored his tone. "We must acknowledge that this map-maker from Genoa shows considerable talent for drawing. A pity, gentlemen, that he does not rest content with his handicraft!"

A titter of mirth ran through the assemblage. Columbus clenched his fists; his face burned, his tongue felt parched.

"There are those among us," de Talavera pursued, "who may wonder why men of science, honored throughout the land, should stoop to argue with an impostor. No matter. Our gracious sovereigns commanded and we obeyed. For what *is* this scheme Señor Columbus has to offer?"

Here the Bishop paused for effect, allowing his mocking glance to flick over the map-maker from Genoa. His thin lips drew back from his teeth. "I hesitate, learned friends, to voice it! It is based on the idea that the earth is shaped as a globe. Ah, already I hear your laughter! It spares me the need of saying anything more."

De Talavera glanced searchingly at Columbus. "We are ready now to hear what *you* have to say, Señor Map-maker."

Slowly Christopher Columbus came to his feet. His glance passed deliberately around the table, resting for a second on each face in turn as if he would engrave them forever in his memory. The anger that had burned in him had subsided. His voice was firm and with purpose as he said: "I recognize my shortcomings, learned gentleman. I am a common man, without crests or ancestors. I was born on the Vico Dritto di Pontecello, in Genoa, and I know the taste of poverty's bread. But I come before you not as a scholar or a noble: I come as a seaman—a seaman who has enjoyed long hours of thought. During those hours I have sought to learn as much as possible about this world, from the maps and calculations of great thinkers, past and present. Also, from my own observations. I have kept my eyes and ears, my mind open."

Gaining confidence, he warmed to the ordeal of facing this challenge. He pointed out that in the dispute of the roundness of the earth, the most learned minds were divided. But, if one accepted the theory, it followed as day follows night that by sailing west, the eastern lands of Cathay and Cipango must be reached. Evidence was indicated in the giant driftwood, the carved timbers that had washed ashore at the Azores.

Brusquely the Bishop of Avila interrupted. "You speak now merely of things of which you have heard. But you cannot show them to us. Are we to consider such hearsay evidence?"

Quickly Columbus came back at him. "These things are on view today in Lisbon. I myself have seen them. You gentlemen can readily inform yourselves of their existence."

"But you do not explain how," the Bishop retorted, "if you sail down the slope of the seas which, as you claim, circle the globe, you expect to sail back up again."

"True," de Deza cut in. "What answer have you to that?"

"It is a matter readily understood by the mariner," Columbus told them boldly. "Those among you who have been to sea know that when the topsails of a ship are on the horizon, the ship itself presently comes into full view. How is that?"

But de Deza swept away his answer with a sneer. "Have you never heard of the mirage? Of the illusions of light and space that trick the eye? To accept these as reality would be to accept the notion of people living on the other side of the earth."

Somewhere another voice was demanding: "We are told that you have already offered these same plans to King John of Portugal. You were refused by him. Is this so?"

"It is true," Columbus answered, "and bitter was my disappointment. But now I see in that refusal the hand of God. It was willed that Ferdinand and Isabella should be endowed with this great opportunity. You have examined my chart, sirs, studied my calculations. But remember—I myself am only an instrument sent by Him who guides us all, to fulfil the promise of that chart. I sail not alone by compass, but by the clear light of faith."

As the last words fell into the silence, there sounded the ringing of the Vesper bell. The seated figures rose. They gathered their robes, drew the cowls about their heads.

Diego de Deza spoke. "We have heard you in

all fairness, Señor Map-maker. The court now goes to its deliberations."

The conference was at an end. With averted heads the hooded figures filed silently from the room. Columbus watched them go. Without hearing their verdict, he knew what it would be. Taut and trembling, he thought of Father Perez, of little Diego waiting eagerly in Palos for word of his success. How could he face them now? How could he bear to tell them that once again he had failed?

Someone grasped him by the arm. "Come along, señor," the porter said gruffly. "It is the hour for locking doors. Or do you prefer to be shut in for the night with the rats? Come along, now."

Columbus straightened his shoulders, flung up his head, and followed.

C H A P T E R   5

Her Majesty
Smiles

THE LEARNED MEN OF SALAMANCA PRO-
nounced the expected verdict: the map-maker's
scheme for finding a route to the Far East by
sailing west had no merit. It was the plot of a
trickster to extort funds from a drained treasury. Let the Genoese quit Spain at the earliest
opportunity!

For Christopher Columbus, the weeks that followed were the most trying of his life. Discredited at every turn, made sport of by noble and commoner alike, he came close to despair. A man of weaker purpose must surely have acknowledged defeat. But in this man's nature there was a toughness of fiber that denied failure. Who won't retreat must go forward! Through many stormy years he had held to his course. He would not swerve from it now. Until he stood before Ferdinand and Isabella themselves, he would not leave Spain!

The unexpected friendship of Don Luis de Santangel gave him comfort in this crisis. That a high-placed grandee, the King's Chancellor, should extend a hand to a low-born foreigner was surprising enough. But de Santangel went further: he sponsored Columbus's cause with wholehearted belief.

"Things have gone badly for you, my poor Christopher," Don Luis said. "But do not despair. A day will come when the wise men of Salamanca will be forced to eat their words. The Queen has promised to hear you as soon as the war ends."

Gloomily the other shook his head. "Promises are made to be broken. Who should know that better than I?"

"Patience but a little longer!"

"I have grown weary with waiting on kings," Columbus answered. "Look you, Don Luis, time is running out like sand in a glass. I have no more years to waste. I am forty-two years old —— My hair is streaked with white!"

"No more so than my own," chided the grandee, "and I am your junior. White hair is a badge of service, good sir. Wear it proudly. As for waiting longer—surely a few more weeks make little difference to one who already has waited so long."

With this, Columbus was forced to rest content.

The royal Court had departed for Granada, the last Moorish stronghold in Spain. In the fortified citadel of the Alhambra, King Boabdil of the Moors was making his final desperate stand.

De Santangel, preparing to join the royal army, insisted that Columbus should accompany him. It were wise, the Chancellor pointed out, to

keep Their Majesties alert to his presence. The
war would not last out the winter. Once it was
won, Columbus was assured of a reception at
Court. The Queen had promised.

Slight as this encouragement was, Columbus
had lived on less. Gratefully he accepted the
Chancellor's invitation. Thus from the humble
lodging of Bensabat, the tailor, he stepped into
the magnificent ducal entourage of Don Luis de
Santangel.

With flying pennants blazoned with blue and
silver, the glittering cavalcade moved south under a late-summer sun. At the head of the column
rode Don Luis in a parade suit of armor, Christopher Columbus at his side. A score of grooms
and henchmen followed, a string of pack-mules
bringing up the rear of the line.

Three days later, Columbus saw the tents of
the royal army sprawled over the plain of Granada like a vast city. Here the King and his
nobles were encamped outside the stubborn gate
of the citadel. Here, too, Queen Isabella, coated
in mail, rode at the side of her warrior husband.

Columbus's heart was high—not with the excitement of battle, but with the awareness that now at last he stood near to the King and Queen. His cause was not yet lost. The optimism that had sustained him for so many years sprang anew in his heart. Surely he would succeed! He looked across the brilliant plain toward the embattled wall of Granada, crumbling stone by stone, and thought: "Only a city to be conquered, yet I offer a whole new world and there is none to heed."

Relentlessly the siege was pressed. Boabdil and his men were stubborn fighters. Summer drew to an end and winter stood on. Christmas came and passed. The besieged fortress trembled under the steady attack. But not until the second day of the New Year did it fall. Boabdil, the Moorish king, cringing like a dog after a beating, rode out to surrender the keys of the city to his conquerors.

Wild joy swept Ferdinand's army. On the Colmares tower the royal banners of Aragon and Castile rose to replace the crescent of Islam. In the crisp sparkle of a January noon the trium-

phant procession of Ferdinand and Isabella
swept through the twin towers that formed the
Gate of Justice and took possession of the fort-
ress-palace of the Alhambra. The struggle of
seven hundred years was at an end. Somewhere
in that shouting victorious company rode Christopher Columbus. Who now, he wondered,
would heed a lowly mariner's prophecy of a new
world? In the excitement of conquest, surely he
would be forgotten.

But he had counted without the help of Don
Luis de Santangel. Not five days passed before
the Chancellor came hurrying to him, flushed
with excitement.

"Good news, O Christopher, my friend!" he
crowed. "Their Majesties are ready to receive
you now. They command your immediate presence in the Alhambra. Ah, I knew it would be
so. The way is clear. Only de Talavera remains
to oppose you——"

"De Talavera?" the other echoed. His enemy!
The way was clear indeed!

"He has been elevated to the post of Archbishop of Granada," Don Luis informed him.
"But you have little to fear. Already he wearies

Their Majesties with his self-importance. Here at last is your great opportunity. Oh, Christopher, you must not fail! Come, we must brush up your doublet. And a stitch or two would not be amiss——"

In the lofty Gold Room in the Alhambra, the Spanish sovereigns had set up their court. Here, by royal command, Christopher Columbus had been summoned to an audience. The marble beauties of the Moorish palace dazzled his eye. Plashing fountains cooled the air; long aisles of columns lost themselves in vanishing-points of obscurity. The vast reception hall that opened off the Court of Lions was hung with silken tapestries from Damascus and Persia. On every side glowed an exotic splendor of mosaic, glazed tile and lacelike carving.

Amid this richness, on a low dais, Isabella of Castile and Ferdinand of Aragon sat in tall chairs of gilded wood. Flanking the noble rulers were the Archbishop of Granada, in purple, the canons and lesser clergy in fine laces and birettas, the glittering noblemen and their ladies in silks and velvets.

In such fine company a man less sure of himself than Christopher Columbus might have been abashed by his now threadbare clothing. He wore it proudly. If ever his hour was to come, this was it.

His eyes took in many details at once: the tall proud King in the gilded armour worn beneath a white mantle with its green cross; the pure oval of Isabella's face, her thoughtful eyes, her faintly encouraging smile that warmed the heart. About the Queen's fair throat a double strand of emeralds caught the light of the sun and threw it back in a blaze of green fire.

The Court notary arose. In a singsong voice he intoned: "Señor Christopher Columbus, of Genoa, seeking audience with Your Majesties, for the purpose of expounding a new route to the Far East."

A murmur ran through the assemblage; for the name of the Genoese map-maker was as familiar to the loftiest knight as to the lowliest herald.

Isabella offered a graceful gesture of invitation. "We have kept you waiting overlong, Señor Columbus," she said, and her low voice was a de-

Isabella

light to the ear. "Your patience commands our admiration. Now that the war at last is over, you shall tell us about your great dream."

In homage Columbus sank to one knee, but the Queen bade him rise. "It is less a dream, Highness," he murmured, "than it is a vision."

"You speak in high confidence, sir."

"I speak in high faith, Your Majesty. A faith that has never left me since first I read the pages of Marco Polo." Columbus's voice warmed with confidence. "You will recall the riches that Polo wrote about! There is more wealth in Cathay than in the combined treasuries of all Europe. He saw houses roofed with gold; children playing with pearls in the mud; princes riding on elephants whose tusks were encrusted with gems beyond a king's ransom. Highness, I pledge my life to lay these treasures at your feet!"

Drily, the practical-minded Ferdinand put in: "We have already heard your project in great detail. You speak as if your dreams were fully realized. But the wise men of Salamanca refused to approve your plan. Do you, perhaps, question their knowledge of science?"

"It is not their knowledge, Sire, that I question," Columbus returned, "but their verdict. They dared not vote to risk three ships—when a thousand ships would not suffice to bring back the treasures of Cathay."

The Archbishop of Granada, Fernando de Talavera, was standing at the Queen's shoulder. His thin lips were parted in a mocking smile.

"Señor Columbus was given a fair hearing at Salamanca," the Archbishop purred. "He amused us with mariners' tales and hearsay. Of evidence to support his theory, he had none. Possibly he has some fresh proof to offer——"

"What man shall have *proof* of lands beyond the western ocean until he makes the voyage there to find out?" Columbus retorted. "Give me but three ships, and by all known laws of science I shall discover the shortest route to the kingdom of the Khan. But I implore Your Majesties to delay no longer! The Portuguese have stolen my charts and calculations. Already their ships may be on the way——"

"But ships," Ferdinand protested, "have to be paid for with more than promises. So do provisions, men, guns. Such an expedition as you propose would cost fifty thousand gold florins, and my treasury is empty!"

"True, Sire, Spain is poor now, but she need not long remain so." Columbus turned toward the Queen. "And what could be more fitting, Highness, than to crown your triumphant victory over the Moors by freeing the Holy Land from the clutch of Islam? Spain alone can make it possible to extend a Christendom that shall give light to the heathen from one end of the earth to the other!"

Isabella was visibly moved by this plea; but before she could speak, de Talavera interrupted artfully. "We have neglected one trifle, Your Majesties," he murmured. "We have not yet asked the gentleman from Genoa what return he expects for his services."

The readiness with which Columbus answered indicated the thought he had given to the matter. In a firm voice he stated: "I ask one-tenth of all gains resulting from my discoveries."

"One *tenth?*" parroted the Archbishop. "You ask the Crown to supply ships, men, provisions, money, while you yourself venture nothing at all, yet you demand one-tenth of the gains?"

"I venture my life, Your Eminence," Columbus reminded him. "I venture my skill as a navigator. And the idea upon which the whole undertaking is based is my own. Is one-tenth so much to ask?"

"Is this the limit of your demands, sir?" asked the King.

"No, Sire. By your leave I ask for the honor of a title: Admiral of the Ocean Seas. Furthermore, I ask for the right to call myself *Don*—and not alone for myself, but for my heirs forever."

"Heaven save us!" exclaimed the King, as if he could not believe his ears. "Such a title would raise you to a rank equal to that of any grandee of Spain."

"Sire, no grandee will ever do more to deserve the honor."

"The man is mad!" cried de Talavera. "I marvel he does not ask for the royal Crown!"

Isabella turned toward the Archbishop with something like anger in her imperious glance. "You overreach yourself, de Talavera," she said coolly. "Señor Columbus stands here at His Majesty's command."

"If I err, Highness," the Archbishop fawned, "it is only out of zeal for your interests. This man's fine dream is but a bubble. Once it bursts, Spain will be the laughing-stock of the world."

"Spain has earned enough honors to insure her against the world's laughter," the Queen retorted. And her voice warmed as she turned toward Columbus. "These, sir, are the extent of your requests?"

"Not quite, Highness," the other answered stubbornly. There was no turning back now. "I ask Vice-royalty over all the lands of my discovery, with a Viceroy's power of life and death."

Astounded silence greeted this remark. Then the King burst out: "By Saint James! What you ask is unheard-of, sir! It is beyond reason."

Quickly Columbus replied: "With less authority I could not fitly represent Your Majesty in foreign lands. My discoveries will be a gift to Spain for all time. Shall I, then, accept a hireling's wage? A man who lays boundless wealth at the feet of his king does not deserve to come out of the affair empty-handed."

"But these riches," the King reminded him, "are still on the other side of your precious globe. You speak as if they were already in hand."

Anxiety beset Don Luis de Santangel as once more he saw success slipping through his friend's fingers. "Could you not demand, less, O Christopher?" he begged. "What you ask is extraordinary——"

"If I speak with unseemly boldness, Don Luis, I crave Their Majesties' pardon. But from my words I cannot turn back. If I am to represent the Crown of Spain before the rulers of Asia, I must be clothed in fitting dignity."

A jarring laugh escaped the Archbishop of Granada. " 'Fitting dignity,' " he jeered. "Observe, Your Majesty, that instead of being content with the wage of a captain, this pauper without a homeland means to amass riches. Nor does he contribute one penny out of his own empty pockets. He will render Castile ridiculous before the whole world."

"Is it true, Columbus," and Ferdinand's tone

was sharp, "that you first offered this same plan
to John of Portugal, and that he refused you?"

Columbus had reserved one trump card for
this very moment. Now, as he played it, he permitted himself to smile. "It is true, Sire," he
answered. "But I have by me a communication
arrived this morning from His Majesty, Charles
VII of France——"

The King's fine eyebrows went up. "Indeed?"
he queried coldly. "And what has our foolish
Charles to say for himself this time?"

"He invites me to go at once to Versailles to
present my proposals to *him*. Shall I enrich
France, Sire, by the very gifts which Spain re-
jects?"

The abrupt silence indicated that Columbus
had scored.

Impatiently Isabella tapped her fingers on the
arm of her chair. Her eyes were clouded with
doubt. "Suppose that Charles—that imbecile—
should profit by our timidity, milord!" she murmured. "The very thought is unbearable."

Hesitant, the King cried out: "But we have
no money to risk on such a gamble. The whole
plan is utterly unsound. Our wisest counsellors

have rejected it. And the honors this man demands for himself——"

Impatiently the Queen brushed aside the words. "The honors and titles depend on his discoveries, milord. If he fails, what has the Crown to lose beyond the cost of equipment? If he succeeds, his demands were small payment indeed."

"Your Majesty," the Archbishop pleaded, "to elevate this adventurer to high station will tarnish the dignity of the Crown. I implore you to consider——"

Coldly Isabella interrupted. "We do not need you, de Talavera, to remind us of the Crown's dignity. 'Adventurer', you say? Is it nothing to be the first to venture upon an unknown ocean?" Her dark eyes flashed at the King. "If the Master of Aragon still cannot make up his mind, then I, Isabella, shall act on behalf of my own kingdom of Castile!"

A gasp of astonishment broke from the throats of the assemblage. No one had ever before heard the Queen thus challenge her consort.

To de Santangel, Isabella said sharply: "What,

Chancellor, do you count as the cost of such an expedition?"

"No ruinous sum," de Santangel answered. "May I remind Your Majesty that the port of Palos is under sentence to supply the Crown with two ships? Fifteen thousand florins would cover the cost of a third."

Slowly the Queen came to her feet, slim and regal. Sunlight, shafting through the columns, struck green fire from the emeralds at her throat. Deliberately she loosened the clasp of the necklace. She dropped it into the Chancellor's palm. "Take these jewels, de Santangel," she said in a firm tone. "Pledge them in my name for the necessary funds." And then a smile of great beauty transformed her face. "Rise, Christopher Columbus! One day your name shall sound in admiration on every man's tongue, to the honor of Spain and to the everlasting glory of God. *Valor y esperanza*, señor!"

Courage and hope . . . Christopher stood with uplifted head. He had won at last. Rank, dignities, authority, rewards were his. He stood as high as the greatest noble in the land. And one day his son, his Diego—waiting so confidently at La Rabida—would enjoy too the right to call himself *Don*.

"Highness," he murmured, and his voice was husky. "From my heart I thank you. I shall not fail. With God's help, I shall lay a new world at your feet!"

Three Ships
Set Sail

DON CHRISTOPHER COLUMBUS, ADMIRAL OF
the Ocean Seas! His return to the monastery of
La Rabida was a triumph. He carried with him
articles of agreement signed by Ferdinand and
Isabella, granting him the high office of Viceroy
and Governor of such lands as he might discover. The articles also bestowed on him and his
heirs a title that was equal to admission into the

nobility of Spain. He who had been jeered at by nobles, mocked in the streets, need bend a knee to no one save his gracious Sovereigns.

More, the Queen had offered special proof of her esteem by appointing Columbus's son as page to the *infante* Don Juan, who was her own son. This appointment, carrying an allowance of 9000 *maravedis,* was an honor given only to the sons of the most distinguished families. There should be no further need to worry about Diego's future.

Happy though he was in being once more with his son, and with his old friend Father Perez, Columbus burned with impatience to complete preparations for his great venture and be off. Rumors of his fearsome voyage, however, swept through the little seaport of Palos, filling the townspeople with dismay. They remembered the Crown sentence, suspended like a sword above their heads, and trembled.

A bright Sunday at the beginning of May found the Church of Saint George crowded. Fishermen, sailors, vineyard workers, shopkeepers, shipowners, caulkers and rope-weavers—all had been summoned to hear a reading of the Royal Decree which the newly appointed Admiral had brought with him from Granada. Here was what the people had feared! They watched in stunned silence as the *Alcalde* rose to face them. Unrolling a scroll of parchment, the magistrate read in loud tone as follows:—

"We, Don Ferdinand and Doña Isabella, by Grace of God the King and Queen of Castile, of Aragon, of Leon, of Granada, of Toledo, of Valencia, of the Balearic Islands, of Gibraltar and of the Canary Islands; Counts of Barcelona; Dukes of Athens and Neopatria; Marquises of Oristan——

To the citizens of Palos:— Well do you know that because of certain acts of smuggling committed by you, in disobedience to Our commands, you were condemned by the Royal Council to equip two vessels at your own expense for the service of the Crown.

We have empowered Don Christopher Columbus, Admiral of the Ocean Seas, to go to certain parts of the western Oceans in Our interests. Within ten days after hearing this summons you are to equip and put at his service two said vessels. Furthermore, you are to sail with him wherever he, on our behalf, shall direct.

Let none of you do otherwise than herein commanded, under pain of Our extreme displeasure and a fine of 10,000 *maravedis* from each of you.

Given in Our City of Granada on the 30th day of April, in the Year of Our Lord 1492.

The *Alcalde* looked severely into the crowd of awe-struck faces that stared at him. He cleared his throat with a rasp. "And may God save Their Majesties," he uttered solemnly.

The hush that followed the reading of the decree told of shocked surprise. Rebellion would come later. The women were terrified. The men were appalled; for not only were they to supply two ships at their own expense, they were commanded to sail with this foreigner into a region from which no one ever had returned.

Palos boasted among its citizens the most daring seamen in Spain; love of the sea was bred in their bones; yet who among them hadn't quaked with fear at tales of the Sea of Darkness? Its waters were known to be black. It threw up horrid monsters powerful enough to drag any vessel down into the deepest gulfs.

And this was the region to which the men of Palos were commanded to sail! They shuddered and crossed themselves. Their women wept for a father, a husband, a brother, a son—as if already these had disappeared from the land of the living. And silently, stubbornly, all vowed in their hearts to place every possible obstacle in the way of this fearful enterprise. Admiral of the Ocean Seas—*tah*! They would never submit to his orders! They would drive this foreign-born "Admiral," who was indebted to the Queen for the very boots he stood in, back to the land of his birth.

In the library at La Rabida, Christopher Columbus looked anxiously into the face of his friend Garcia Fernandez, the town's physician.

"What luck, my friend?" He had been asking this same question, now, for a week.

Gloomily Fernandez shook his head. "There is not a man in Palos who will sail with you,

Don Christopher. Nor in the neighboring towns of Huelva or Moguer. I have done my best to persuade them. But the Sea of Darkness has fixed a terror on them."

Columbus uttered a cry. "For years, fools have stood in my way," he fumed. "Shall I draw back now for cowards? Never! Somehow I shall find three ships and the men to sail them, if it be necessary to empty the jails of criminals!"

Father Perez was aghast. "Sail with a crew of murderers and bandits?" he exclaimed. "Are you daft? You will have troubles enough, Don Christopher, without adding mutiny."

The good father was sorely troubled. Each day he had gone into the village among the people. By appealing first to one, now another, he had sought to raise their spirits and convince them that the Admiral's voyage would be certain of success, that the stories of the Sea of Darkness were old wives' tales. He talked to ears that were deaf.

"If only Martin Pinzon were here," cried Fernandez, springing up. "His word carries more weight in town than any man's. The people will

listen to him. I do believe they would follow
him to the gates of Hades."

"Let us hope we don't sail that far," was
Columbus's wry answer. "When is Pinzon expected to return from the Canaries?"

"Alas, who can say? Already his ship is over-
due."

There was no knowing what unforeseen disaster might have overtaken the wealthy ship-
owner. And every passing day was one more day
lost. Bitterly Columbus realized that the solu-
tion of each problem only presented a fresh one
to be solved.

The fears of the townspeople rose to angry
excitement. Threats were made against the life
of this Genoese "Admiral" who would lead the
men of Palos to their death. Alarmed, Father
Perez urged Columbus to remain in hiding at
La Rabida until the feeling against him died
away. But daily the Admiral went fearlessly into
the town to inspect ships lying in the harbor,
and to try to win the confidence of men who
turned their backs as he passed.

He soon found the shipowners themselves banded stubbornly against him. True, they admitted, the town held itself answerable for damages; but their ships were certain to be lost on such a senseless voyage. Who would be answerable then? And if it came to taking action against the Crown, they would be ruined by lawsuits before they ever received a *maravedi* in payment. No ship in existence was seaworthy enough to survive such a voyage as this mad foreigner proposed!

Nor were the port authorities slow to act with the shipowners in stopping Columbus's project. Any man who could invent an excuse for taking his ship out of port was supplied with a commission. Day by day the harbor grew more deserted. Seamen who feared being pressed into service, disappeared mysteriously and their families claimed to know nothing of their whereabouts.

It seemed that there wasn't a single vessel to be had at any price, nor a crew to be mustered. Matters came to a standstill. The unhappy *Alcalde,* trembling for his own safety, was obliged to send a report of the deadlock to King Ferdinand.

Thus some weeks passed in tensest excitement. Had the King and Queen repented of their folly and abandoned this foolhardy venture? It soon became clear that they had not.

With an angry flourish of trumpets a royal messenger rode into Palos. He bore a decree issued to all city authorities on the coast of Andalusia: they were to seize suitable ships at once, wherever found, and compel owners and crews to place themselves under command of the Admiral. Prison awaited the man who refused. In addition, the villagers must pay the daily expenses of the royal messenger until all preparations were complete for Columbus's departure.

Affairs had reached a crisis during which anything might happen. When the caravel *Pinta* arrived in port from Guinea, and the royal messenger ordered her seized in the name of the Crown, the threats against the Admiral's life were doubled.

At this moment, Martin Alonzo Pinzon fortunately returned from the Canaries with his caravel, the *Niña*. Now, the name Pinzon was respected and feared along the entire seaboard of Andalusia. Martin and his two brothers—Vincent and Francisco—were known to be bold and expert navigators. They were, moreover, shrewd men of affairs. Most families in town were under some financial obligation to the Pinzons. If they should lend the weight of their approval to Columbus's undertaking, it seemed certain that the men of Palos would follow their lead.

Martin Alonzo sized up the situation at a glance. Here was a venture after his own heart! No one but a fool, however, rushed into an enterprise without first computing his own profit. When he discovered that Christopher Columbus had been awarded the highest of titles, plus a generous grant from the Crown, he hurried to La Rabida, promising that all would be well.

"Already you have the *Pinta* in hand, my Admiral," he said with a chuckle, "and I'll wager a florin to a *maravedí* that your second vessel will reach port by tomorrow evening."

These words were mystifying. "Tomorrow——?"

"Aye," and the other grinned, enjoying his

joke. "Two days out of port I passed my old rival, Juan de la Cosa, master of the *Gallego*. She will cross the bar of Saltes on tomorrow's tide. If the King's men are warned, they can be waiting to seize her. Congratulations, my friend! The *Gallego* is as good as yours. A seaworthy ship, if somewhat slow."

And that was the way it happened. Drifting into the Rio Tinto, the *Gallego* was seized in the name of the Crown before her hawsers were securely knotted, thereby affording Martin Alonzo a joke that he greatly enjoyed. What better way was there to remove a rival lawfully, than in the King's name?

To Columbus's eye, the *Gallego* was too deep of draught to be practical for sailing off unknown coasts, where a ship should be as flat-bottomed as possible to clear uncharted reefs and sandbars. But beggars could not be choosers. Changing the *Gallego's* name to *Santa Maria*, the Admiral declared her his flagship.

Now he had two sturdy three-masters, but where were the men to sail them? Like fog before a rising sun the crews of both vessels had vanished into thin air. Their families vowed by all the Saints that only Satan knew what had become of them! To persuade the men to return, the Admiral posted wages at the same rate as on ships-of-war, with four months' payment in advance. He promised that the Crown would forgive any civil or criminal charges against all who answered the King's call. But not a man appeared in response.

"They'll show up," declared Martin Pinzon. "I have ways of seeing that men who owe me anything do as I ask. But, *amigo*, have you given thought to your third vessel? Where is she to be found?"

"I have been told I may offer two thousand crowns for a third ship," the Admiral said. "But the port is empty! I know not where to turn. It may be necessary for me to sail with only two——"

Pinzon appeared to be giving the matter deep thought: he pursed his lips and made a tent of his fingers. "It were madness to sail with less than three," he mused. "If misfortune should overtake one ship, the other would be left to her own resources and obliged to carry both crews."

Suddenly Pinzon's face lighted; his teeth flashed in an honest, open smile. He slapped his thigh a mighty blow. "I have it! Just the vessel for you! My own little *Niña*—a sweet ship. Only a hundred tons burden, true, but she'll show her heels to the *Pinta* or the *Santa Maria* any day. You may have her for two thousand crowns, my Admiral, and there's a bargain!"

It was typical of Pinzon's shrewdness that he should have disposed of a rival's ship under cover of action by the King, only to reserve his own for purchase. By such means had he attained wealth and consequence.

There remained the task of re-fitting the three ships that now stood at Columbus's disposal. But immediately another snag was encountered: sullen workmen used every possible means to delay the task. In this they were encouraged by friends and relatives. It was necessary to be constantly on guard against their tricks.

One morning as Columbus came upon the caulkers at work on the *Pinta*, he discovered that they were rigging the rudder in such fashion that it would work out of place in the first heavy sea. By this means, the Admiral would be forced to send the *Pinta* back before she had sailed many miles from home port. Angered at such a trick, Columbus ordered the work done over again.

The men pretended to obey; but when the Admiral's back was turned, they ran off in a body and hid themselves in the hills. Where were more workmen to be found to replace them?

Often of an evening, returning to La Rabida, Columbus found himself weighted down by such a burden of care that his friend Father Perez had difficulty in comforting him. At such moments, his three ships seemed sadly unequal to the dangers ahead. Suppose his calculations should prove to be wrong? He planned to carry provisions to last for six months; but if, at the end of that time, he hadn't reached the kingdom of the Great Khan—what then? He and his men would die of starvation and thirst! Then, impatient with himself, he brushed these doubts aside.

His joy returned on the morning when Martin Alonzo, with his brothers Vincent and Francisco, declared that they too would join the expedition. Martin would command the

Pinta, with Francisco as pilot. Vincent would captain the *Niña*. Columbus himself, of course, would be in command of the flagship, *Santa Maria*. No plan could have pleased the Admiral more.

By nightfall, the news had reached the hills where the men were in hiding. The Pinzons' decision had more effect than all the penalties threatened by the Crown; for one by one the seamen drifted back into the town. Still fearful, they knew that further resistance was useless. No wise man defied the Pinzons for long!

Within a week a hundred-odd sailors had been mustered. Of these, sixty were to ship with the *Santa Maria*, thirty with the Pinta, the remainder with the *Niña*. Capable mates—or pilots, as they were called—were found for each vessel. It pleased Columbus that his friend the physician, Garcia Fernandez, would sail with him; for of all the ships' company, the Admiral alone was an outsider, a foreigner. The personnel numbered, too, an interpreter named Luis de Torres, whose languages included Greek, Arabic and Hebrew, Spanish, Portuguese and Italian. It was thought that his assistance would be invaluable in the Indies! There was an assayer of precious metals, a carpenter, a cooper or barrel-maker, and a smith. Casks of trade goods were loaded aboard—beads, hawkbells, and many small trinkets. Food; water, spare sails and spars; firearms and ammunition. The *Santa Maria* carried heavy cannon called lombards, and lighter guns known as falconets. Their projectiles of stone and iron would serve as ballast.

On the second day of August the little fleet lay at anchor in the Rio Tinto, ready for departure. On the evening of that day the Admiral and his officers, together with the foremast hands, trudged up the hill to the monastery of La Rabida. There Father Perez gave them solemn warning of the great task that lay before them as pioneers of Christianity in the New World. Then he blessed them all. Many bowed their heads in anguish, for it seemed as if the pious ceremony were only a preparation for the last journey from this world to the other life.

Thoughtfully, the men returned to their ships, through cobbled streets where women and children set up sorrowful cries. Dark and accusing looks were cast upon the Admiral of the Ocean

Seas as he strode through the weeping throng. More than one woman, mourning her men as lost, made horns of her fingers, as one who would ward off the Evil Eye.

The tide stood at the ebb. The fateful hour had come. The caravels tugged at their anchors. Columbus and his officers were rowed out to their respective ships. The seamen followed.

The sun was just rising behind the promontory of La Rabida as the Admiral mounted the high poop of the *Santa Maria*. Below him, amidships, a trumpeter sent out a golden blast. With that sound Christopher Columbus shouted his first command:

"Hoist anchor! Cast loose all sail!"

The boatswain's whistle shrilled. The capstan clanked. To a rousing chantey the anchor broke water and was tripped aboard. The yards were braced sharp up. Ropes whined in the sheaves. For a second the *Santa Maria* quivered as the tide reached for her with hungry fingers. Her canvas filled. Sail after sail, emblazoned with the Cross of Malta, glistened in the rising sun. The flags of Castile and Aragon floated from the tallest mast. The Admiral's pennon whipped from the mizzen. From the other ships drifted echoing commands . . .

Then with the *Pinta* and the *Niña* crowding her wake, the flagship came abreast of La Rabida. Columbus looked back toward the land. He beheld the low white-walled mass of the monastery, the figures of the lay-brothers standing with clasped hands. He saw, too, old Father Perez standing straight as a drawn sword. Then he saw a smaller figure detach itself from the others and race along the promontory, in parallel with the ship's passage. Columbus's heart tightened. Diego, his son . . . Above the cry of wind and seabirds came the youthful call: *"Padre! Padrecito! Adios . . . Adios . . ."*

The Admiral's pennon dipped in salute.

The *Santa Maria* came about smoothly in answer to command. Crossing the choppy currents of the bar of Saltes, she pointed her stem to the open sea—bound toward a destiny akin to that of the immortals.

CHAPTER 7

The Sea of Darkness

WITH ALL SAIL SET AND DRAWING HAND-
somely, the three ships romped across the swells.
A course was laid for Grand Canary. From there
the little fleet would head due west—sailing into
the Sea of Darkness until, God willing, it should
at last raise land.

From that first hour, in the quiet of his cabin,
Christopher Columbus began to write the log

of the *Santa Maria*. No detail should be too insignificant to record. Winds, birds, currents, fishes, clouds; the distance made each day with various combinations of sail; all would find their way into his journal, for the benefit of his Sovereigns and for his own glory.

For the first time "Admiral of the Ocean Seas" seemed more than an empty title. Here at last was a chance to prove that by imagination and courage, by skill and daring, an unknown region of the globe would be laid bare to the eyes of men. What a sense of happiness possessed Columbus as he stood on the quarterdeck, directing the steering of his ship by the feel of the wind against his cheek! How good it was to leave the land behind!

But the uncertain temper of the crew made itself felt even above the excitement of the moment. Caught between threats of punishment by the Crown, and by the displeasure of the Pinzons, the men had suffered themselves to be dragged from home. If, in desperation, they should one day band together and insist on turning back, what would become of this great enterprise? Fear of the Unknown was common to all. When the prow of their ships pointed west from Ferro (the most outlying island of the Canaries) they would leave not only the familiar coasts of Spain and Africa, but all they had ever heard of as being the outermost edge of the world. If the wise men of Salamanca had refused to believe in the Admiral's vision, was it surprising that ignorant sailors should feel likewise?

Nor did it allay the fears of the superstitious to remember that they had sailed from Palos on a Friday—a day that many believed to bring bad luck.

Perhaps that is why, three days later, they saw a sign of ill luck to come when Martin Pinzon's vessel signaled that her rudder was broken. Under a towering press of sail the *Pinta* had held the lead. Now she fell rapidly astern. A fair gale was blowing and the Admiral could not go to Pinzon's assistance. But the clever Martin Alonzo was able to meet the emergency. Shortening sail, he contrived a jury rig for the rudder, enabling his ship to stagger the remaining miles to Grand Canary. There full repairs could be made. Recalling the day he had come upon the sullen workmen in the shipyard, Columbus was certain that the broken rudder was part of a scheme to make him return to Spain. He fumed with anger. Now precious days would be lost while the *Pinta* was being re-conditioned.

The Admiral profited somewhat by the delay, however, for he was determined to have the *Niña's* lateen, or triangular sails, altered to square-rig. From the beginning he had viewed the former with misgiving, knowing that a lateen-rigged caravel was handicapped in close-hauled sailing.

These operations took a full three weeks. Not until the sixth day of September was all in readiness. But here a fresh disaster threatened the little fleet: a caravel arriving from the island of Ferro reported three Portuguese ships-of-war cruising in that region, bent on seizing Columbus and his fleet. The danger was grave. The Admiral could not hope to defend himself against attack. Sail must be made at once if he was to slip past the watchdogs of the Portuguese king. He gave immediate orders to that effect.

At sunset, close-hauled in a spanking breeze,

the *Pinta* and the *Niña* fled in the wake of the flagship. As they passed under the forbidding peak of Teneriffe, the volcano could be seen in full eruption. Never had the crew beheld such a terrifying sight! Columns of smoke billowed to the sky, shot through with darting flame. Rivers of molten fire ran down the slopes of the mountains. The sky was forked with lightning.

Appalled, the men were convinced that here at the very threshold of the Sea of Darkness they beheld a foretaste of the future. The force of the wind drove the three caravels close in to the shores of Ferro—the very spot where the Portuguese warships were reported to be cruising. It seemed to Columbus that he had fallen right into the wolf's mouth.

But suddenly the wind shifted dead astern, and quickened to a twelve-knot gale. Tiny Ferro, last outpost of the known world, dropped rapidly from sight. Columbus had slipped safely past the enemy.

With the disappearance of land, panic swept through the three ships. The empty sky met the empty sea in an unbroken line of horizon. The caravels were the moving center of a limitless circle of water, lost and forsaken. Even the most seasoned sailors, who many times had faced storm and death, were seen to weep. Where and how would they die? What horrid monsters would rise from the sea to devour them?

In the quiet of his cabin, marking entries in the Journal, Columbus heard the men's cries and his heart was troubled.

So it was scarcely a surprise when Alfredo, the boatswain, informed him: "There's bad talk in the fo'c'sle, Don Admiral. The men would have speech with you."

"Trouble afoot already?" Columbus demanded.

"I fear so, Don Admiral."

Bare-headed, with the wind ruffling his white-streaked mane, Columbus strode to the rail of the quarterdeck, where a flight of steps led down to the waist. Below, a group of men huddled together, their weathered faces turned upward. A rumble of protest made itself heard as a threat.

The Admiral raised his hand for silence, but one shrill voice defied him: "Where are you leading us, O man of Genoa? Tell us that!"

Columbus stared back at the speaker. "Fool!" he answered. "I lead you out of poverty into wealth, out of misery into glory."

"Glory?" the voice shot back. "Why should we risk our lives for a crazy gamble?"

"Does my life mean nothing to me, that I risk it too?" cried Columbus. "Gamble, you call it! What are your lives worth weighed against the chance of ease and plenty, of honor and fame? I know what I am about. Do you suppose Their Majesties would have trusted me with these ships had I not persuaded them of that fact?"

"But *where* do you take us——?"

Sternly the Admiral answered: "Seven hundred leagues to the west lies the island of Cipango. There the very houses are roofed with gold. You will return to Spain the most envied of men. Your children shall never know the strain of toil, the pang of hunger. Have faith in me! Get yourselves to your tasks, men. God has smiled on us. He will lead us safe to home port —to be praised and rewarded."

So commanding were his tone and manner, so

convincing his words, that as he finished speaking a cheer broke from the very throats which a moment before had rumbled with threats.

But Columbus was not deceived. He knew that the *Santa Maria* was a floating arsenal needing only a spark to produce an explosion. He had given instructions to the commanders of the other two ships that, in case they should become separated, they were to continue due west for a distance of seven hundred leagues, at which point they could expect to sight land.

Yet some margin for error must be allowed. Having stated positively the location of Cipango, Columbus could not afford to be wrong. To this end he worked out a little trick which might lighten the fears of his men. In his secret Journal he marked the correct distance sailed each day; but in the public register, open to the inspection of all, he reduced the actual distance by many miles.

For instruments, the *Santa Maria* carried only a compass and an astrolabe, by which the latitude could be determined. But the Admiral could only guess at his longitude and he measured time by an hour-glass. Since exact reckoning was impossible, the Pinzons would be unable to dispute his calculations even if they suspected they were being fooled.

Scarcely had this trick been established when a more alarming problem presented itself. Some two hundred leagues at sea, Columbus discovered that the magnetic needle of the compass, which always had pointed to the north star, showed a deviation of several degrees. Such a thing had never been heard of. Seated in his cabin, brooding over the Journal, the worried man wrote:

"Yesterday, into the evening, the needles varied a whole quarter to the northwest. This morning they stood still farther away. I have tested my observations again and again—with the same result. What is the cause? How shall I hide this alarming fact from the men?"

Surely Martin Pinzon in the *Pinta*, and Vincent in the *Niña*, must have observed the same deviation! Would they have the wit to conceal it? If the magnetic needle could not be trusted, if the very stars were beginning to waver, what was there to depend on in this boundless waste of water? In that moment Columbus recalled tales

told by old seamen—stories of magnetic mountains that drew every bit of iron out of ships so
that they fell apart. Could this disaster be in
store for him?

It remained for the boatswain, Alfredo, to
discover the needle's deviation and spread the
bad tidings to the crew. Here was proof, if such
were needed, that they had sailed beyond the
boundaries of the natural world. Now indeed
were they doomed.

"Look for yourself, Don Admiral!" Alfredo
cried, pointing to the compass. "Are we to sail
forever in this sea when the needle has lost its
power to guide us home?"

A score of angry voices from amidships
echoed the question.

Columbus's mind raced forward and back to
meet the emergency. Somehow he must satisfy
the men with an explanation of this strange thing
which he himself did not understand, for any
answer was better than none at all. He stared
into the compass, thinking. Then suddenly he
flung back his head and burst into laughter. The
men stared at him, as if he had gone daft.

"You, Alfredo," he roared. "Lubberly idiots,

all of you! What manner of seamen do you call yourselves? Why do you find *the needle* at fault because it no longer points at the North Star?"

The boatswain gaped stupidly. "But why not, Don Admiral? The needle has always pointed north—until now."

Again Columbus roared with laughter, as if enjoying some huge joke. "You lubberly fools! What a crew for an Admiral of the Ocean Seas! The fault lies not with the needle, you numskulls."

"Then what——?"

"The star itself moves. There is your answer."

"But——"

"Observe how the star makes its way across the sky," the other interrupted, "while the needle remains constant to a point in the north invisible to the eye. How could the compass guide us if it, too, moved with the star? Stop chattering with fear! Must you be cowards as well as fools?"

Momentarily the men were silent as they thought about this astonishing statement. Taking advantage of their confusion, the Admiral ordered them back to their tasks.

But Alfredo, more intelligent than his mates, stammered: "In all my years at sea I have never seen the like——"

"All *your* years at sea?" Columbus scoffed. "You were a puling babe when I had already crossed the Mediterranean a score of times. Keep an eye to the course now and no more nonsense."

"Yes, Don Admiral——"

Some days later, hopes were revived by the appearance of a tern and a wagtail, which hovered above the ship for some time. Birds of such species were thought never to fly far from land. But by nightfall, when the birds had disappeared, an unexpected sight in the skies threw all hands into consternation. The sea was calm, the air still, the heavens bright with stars, when suddenly a streak of fire darted across the sky and disappeared into the sea. It seemed so close that the men thought they heard it hissing through space. Its bright wake lingered for many seconds. The strange sight struck awe into minds prepared to be alarmed by any unusual event. The heavenly bodies were plunging into the sea!

It was shortly after this that the first patches of sea-grass were noticed, extending as far as the eye could reach. When, on one of these patches, a live crab was discovered, some of the men insisted that land could not be far off.

The three ships had overtaken the trade-winds: favorable breezes that follow the sun's course, blowing steadily from east to west. There would be no need to change a sail for days to come. But even this friendly wind became a source of alarm, for it blew always from the same direction: away from home. How could a ship ever sail back against such a wind? She might tack forever and ever, until her men died of famine and her bones fell apart. . . .

Each sun as it rose seemed hotter than that of the preceding day. The face of the ocean became a blazing disk. It was whispered that the ship's stores were beginning to run low, that the rats were deserting the hold. The bread was riddled by weevils, the wine had soured, the drinking water was foul in the casks. Men tightened their belts and cast dark looks in the direction of the quarterdeck, where Columbus stood.

Aboard the *Pinta* the same spirit prevailed.

Martin Pinzon was a man of reckless will with little liking for moving in file with his companions. As eager as the Admiral to make discoveries on his own account, he could not forget that Queen Isabella had offered a yearly pension of 10,000 *maravedis* to the man who first sighted land. Martin Alonzo was unwilling to allow this prize to slip through his fingers.

On the morning of the eighteenth day of September Pinzon signaled to the *Santa Maria* that he had seen a vast flock of birds flying westward, and he proposed to follow them under full sail. Land could not be far distant. Remembering that the Portuguese had discovered most of their islands by following the flight of birds, Columbus reluctantly allowed Pinzon to have his way. Any division of his small fleet was a serious matter. No one knew what lay ahead and many a ship had been wrecked in the breakers of an unknown coast. The *Pinta* raced away, westward, while the Admiral gazed anxiously after her.

But by evening she was back again in her accustomed place. Martin Alonzo had sighted nothing more exciting than the same measureless miles of floating green meadow.

It required constant watching on Columbus's part to make certain that the helmsmen never permitted the ship's course to fall off. He slept fitfully, but seemed to have little need of sleep. He appeared hardly to know what he ate, or to care. From time to time he talked across the water with Martin or Vincent Pinzon; but for the rest, he remained silent, and alone.

Each new day brought fresh evidence of land in the offing: pelicans flew about the ship; once a sea-swallow allowed itself to be caught by hand.

The stretches of sea-grass had become as dense as a swamp. With difficulty the vessels made their way through it. The men had heard of ships being caught and imprisoned in ice, but never anything like this! Were they to run aground hundreds of leagues from all assistance? Soundings were taken, but at two hundred fathoms no bottom could be found.

At night, when the foremast hands lay sweltering in their bunks, when black silence enveloped them and little wavelets gnawed like rats at the ship's planking, fear touched with clammy fingers one man after another. They crossed themselves, buried their heads and growled threats at the foreign-born "Admiral" whose mad folly was leading them to destruction. Their voices merged into a babel of anger.

"Where are the promised lands now? Where the mountains of gold? We shall all perish in this foul swamp!"

"By the Admiral's count we've already sailed five hundred leagues. How much farther does he mean to take us?"

"Ho, by the Admiral's count! We are fools to trust the word of a madman."

"But there must be land somewhere. The birds, the sea-grass——"

"*Tah!* That story has been told too often. We've been tricked with fine words. This dog of a Genoese has traded on the Queen's good faith. But the men of Salamanca said from the first it was madness——"

"Then why don't we do something about it? If we pull together, mates, what have we to lose? Why not throw this fine Admiral into the sea? We can say he fell overboard and who'll be the wiser? Let us act now—before it is too late! This very night. Heave him to the sharks!"

"Stay, brother. The time is not yet ripe . . ."

On such a note did many a night end and many a new day begin.

Sunset, on the twenty-fifth of September, found Columbus in his cabin. He was falsifying the record of the day's run. Scarce a cable's length to starboard the *Pinta* was running free before the tradewind; when suddenly a loud cry, winging across the waves, brought the Admiral bounding to his feet.

"Tierra! Tierra oho!"

Land! Land in sight!

Even as Columbus raced for the companion-way he heard his men burst into a joyous hymn of praise. The crews of the *Pinta* and the *Niña*, too, lifted their voices in thanks to the Almighty. A profound gratitude surged in the Admiral's heart, tightened his throat. High in the rigging, Alfredo shouted that he too could see land—some twenty-five leagues to the south-west.

"Stand by to shorten sail!" cried Columbus. "Bring her round close-hauled on the larboard tack!"

The *Santa Maria* responded instantly to command. Her sister ships did likewise. In their joy, many sailors flung themselves into the sea, swimming sportively beside the ship.

Darkness shut down. That night men danced and sang on deck. No one closed an eye. No one doubted that morning would see an end to this endless voyage. The wealth of the Indies lay on the horizon!

But by sunrise the vision of land had disappeared, swallowed in the mystery of the sea.

This cruel disappointment plunged all the men into despair. By the public log, the *Santa Maria* had sailed five hundred and twenty leagues from Ferro. Fortunately, only Columbus knew how far short of the truth this reckoning was. His secret Journal gave the figure at seven hundred and seven leagues!

But ever the ships plowed westward. Birds too small for long-sustained flight came and disappeared at sunset. Fishes were seen of a kind which never swim far from the coast. Branches with fruit still clinging floated on the sluggish tide. The *Niña* signaled that her men had seen a reed and a staff in the water—a small staff which appeared to have been cut with iron. The crew of the *Pinta* reported a branch of thorn with fresh berries on it.

Day and night, with mind and heart intent, all hands searched the horizon in every direction. Each distant cloud took on the shape of land. Every little while, first from one vessel then another, was heard the joyful but false cry: "*Tierra!* Land!"

At seven hundred leagues the Admiral had confidently counted on reaching Cipango. For the first time doubt began to gnaw at his peace of mind. Could he have made some mistake in his calculations? When a large flock of petrels appeared above the ship, he determined that same evening to follow their homeward flight. This decision brought great rejoicing. But though the birds were pursued stubbornly into the west, nothing was seen of land that day, nor the next, nor the one following. . . .

The anxiety of the crew burned like a fever. Something must happen soon. The men had lost faith in signs. Mutiny hung by a trigger balance.

The storm burst when the Admiral scolded the helmsman for allowing the ship to fall off course. Quick as a snake's striking, the sailor's hand darted to his belt. A knife flashed. But Columbus side-stepped the blow. Then he sprang forward, seized the man by his doublet. With a powerful swing he hurled him bodily down the steps. The sailor struck the midships deck with a crash.

Half a dozen of the foremast hands had watched the encounter. Now they raced for the quarterdeck steps, shouting as they ran. Suddenly they halted; for the Admiral had swung an arquebus on its swivel so that it commanded the approach to the poop. They stared into a black and threatening gun muzzle.

"Back, you scum, or I fire!" cried Columbus.

"Hear us, Don Admiral!" a voice shouted defiantly. "Holy Spirit! Would you shoot defenceless men?"

"Since when is a man defenceless with a knife in his hands?" the other flung back. "Say what you want from where you stand. I shoot to kill the first among you who mounts those steps."

It was Alfredo who responded: "They demand that you put about, Don Admiral. Return to Spain——"

A score of voices took up the cry: "Aye! Put about while there's still time. We demand it!"

"You demand?" the Admiral cried scornfully. "Be silent there and listen to me. Before this ship puts about she will reach Cipango. And while one plank of her floats, *I am in command!* Is that clear to you?"

"Admiral," Alfredo protested weakly, "they have made up their minds. Already they have sailed farther than you bargained. They will go no more——"

"Then over the side with them," Columbus thundered. "Let them swim back to Spain. This ship does not put about!"

The gaping threat of the arquebus, the blaze of purpose in the Admiral's eyes momentarily induced silence. Then one voice whined: "You are carrying us to our death, Admiral. No ship can return against winds that blow ever westward."

"God grant me patience to deal with such an idiot," Columbus ground out. "Don't you know that when a belt of wind blows from one quarter, a similar wind blows from an opposite parallel? God willing, by such a wind we shall re-

turn to Spain one day. You have been privi-
leged to travel farther into the Ocean Sea than
any man before you. Now you would have me
put about and go home to say: 'Let someone else
find the way. We failed!' You cowards! Get
back to your tasks like men, while still you live."

Once again the Admiral's will prevailed.
Scowling but silent, the men returned to their
posts. But Columbus knew in his heart that a
day would come when words or threats would
no longer avail. Before that day, God grant, he
would sight land . . .

Not an eye closed that night. The Admiral
took his accustomed stand on the high poop. He
ordered the stern lanterns extinguished and with
sleepless eyes sought to look into the darkness
ahead.

Then, two hours before midnight, the miracle
happened. A far-off light struck his eyes. It
wavered once or twice, moving quickly on the
horizon, like a fisherman's boat rising and falling
on the waves. His heart hammered. But he
dared not cry out: *"Land!"* He distrusted himself and his senses. He summoned the boatswain.

"Your eyes are sharp, Alfredo," he whispered.

"Tell me what you see yonder——" Even as he spoke, the light disappeared.

The boatswain strained into the darkness. "I see nothing, Don Admiral."

The light had reappeared. "Look again!"

"Ah, yes, *yes!* A light. Over there——"

"Quiet! You are certain, Alfredo?"

"But yes, Admiral! It is gone now, yet I saw it, on my oath——"

Surely this was no trick of the eyes! Alfredo had seen it too. Somewhere ahead in darkness were human beings, inhabited land. But so often had hopes been falsely raised, so often dashed, that Columbus commanded Alfredo to keep silent. They stood shoulder to trembling shoulder, staring into the dark.

Hour after hour passed. The sand-glass under the helmsman's lantern showed that it was two o'clock in the morning. The hulls of the other two ships loomed vaguely to starboard and in the east the line of the horizon was clearly defined.

Then from the *Pinta* came a flash of flame, a roar of cannon. The long-awaited signal! Land in sight.

Almost instantaneously from the crosstrees came the ringing cry: *"Tierra! Tierra oho!"*

There in the west, green and fair, lay an island.

Who can tell what Christopher Columbus felt at that moment? The long waiting was at an end. The dream had materialized. In his ears rang the voices of his men singing *Te Deum Laudamus*—Almighty God we praise Thee. Voices from the other ships joined in singing the solemn hymn.

Driven by the favoring wind, the three caravels clipped across the equatorial currents, and the hush-hush of their cut-water shattered the morning stillness of the world.

The day was Friday, the twelfth of October, Fourteen Hundred and Ninety-Two.

CHAPTER 8

How Green the Land!

To EYES WEARY OF THE SEA, THE LAND-
fall looked as green as the heart of an emerald.
To ears dulled by the slat and bang of canvas,
the high-bursting surf on the reef came as a cry
of welcome. The men who lined the bulwarks of
the three ships, or clung like flies to the rigging,
feasted on the sight of the living land. After
seventy-one days at sea, it promised fresh food

and water, rest and enjoyment. To their commander-in-chief, however, it spoke of destiny
fulfilled and of duty yet to perform.

With upflung head Christopher Columbus
gazed long and searchingly at this fragment of
earth over which, by royal decree, he was Viceroy and Governor-General. He had no doubt
that it was the gateway to the kingdom of the
Grand Khan—one of the many isles with which
Marco Polo had dotted the archipelago of the
Indies.

Sail was shortened as the little squadron came
up into the wind. The leadsman of the *Santa
Maria,* resigned to finding no bottom with his
forty-fathom line, suddenly got a sounding—
a measure almost unnecessary, for the glass-clear
water could be sounded by the eye.

"By the mark seven!" called the leadsman.
"By the mark six . . . By the mark five-and-a-
half . . ."

"Anchors—let go!"

The splash from the bows of each ship sent
clouds of gulls whirling and screaming above the
surf. The *Santa Maria* swung to her hawser.

With feverish eyes Columbus surveyed the

scene. Palms strange to his sight lined the beach. Behind them, tier upon tier, rose the jungle: pines of great size, giant bamboos, flowers as brightly colored as the parrots that flitted through the trees. The air was as balmy as spring in Andalusia and it came to the ship laden with nameless perfumes.

As he stood there, tranced, the Admiral saw graceful figures darting from cover to cover among the foliage—naked savages, Indians, yet scarcely duskier than the Spaniards themselves.

Longboats were made ready to go ashore. Some of the sailors, armed with muskets and crossbows, already had transformed themselves into soldiers. Columbus girded on his sword and donned the mantle of a military commander-in-chief, as became an emissary to the Grand Khan. A golden cross gleamed on his breast; his left hand gripped the standard of Castile. He went over the side into the waiting boat, followed by the notary Rodrigo de Escovedo, the master-at-arms Aranda, his pilot Cosa, Alfredo and a handful of others.

From the *Pinta* and the *Niña* came boats bearing the Pinzon brothers and their followers. It was they who carried the flags of the expedition: white banners emblazoned with a green cross. The oarsmen pulled toward a point on shore where an inlet allowed safe passage through the pounding surf.

As the prow of his boat grated the coral shore, the Admiral sprang overside into the shallows. Eagerly he strode up the beach, then fell to his knees and kissed the earth. His followers knelt behind him while he offered up a prayer of thanksgiving. Every voice trembled in singing the *Salve Regina.*

Then the Admiral rose up and grasped Martin Pinzon by the hand. "Blessed be God for all His mercies," he cried fervently. "I know not what this place may be, but I have found land by sailing West! It is vindication of all that I have endured."

"God's truth, but that is so!" the other agreed, pumping his commander's hand. In the excitement of the moment Pinzon forgot the many grudges he had been storing up against his commander. "He laughs longest who laughs last. Generations to come will laugh at the wise-acres of Salamanca."

All the men crowded round as Columbus struck the royal standard into the earth. Taking formal possession of this land in the name of his Sovereigns, the Admiral drew his sword, raised his head and cried: "Land of my salvation, I christen thee *San Salvador*, after our Saviour."

The notary Escovedo drew up the deed of recording, while those grouped on the beach solemnly set their hands in witness of the Admiral's proclamation.

Meanwhile, the savages—or Indians, as Columbus miscalled them—were gathering rapidly in the protective jungle: a thousand or more. Curiosity overcame caution as they peered, fascinated, at the strange human beings kneeling on the beach. The three great birds which had borne these odd visitors were already folding their white wings. Surely they had flown straight from heaven!

Slowly, the Indians edged forward from cover. Though they were armed with bone-tipped spears, they were not hostile nor were they afraid. They were soft-spoken, eager to please, and their eyes were gentle. Awe stamped their faces. Some had painted their naked bodies; a few of the older men wore pins of yellow metal in their noses, recognized instantly as virgin gold.

By friendly gestures Columbus encouraged them to approach. If the Indians did not understand the words he used, there was no mistaking the warmth of his smile. A cask of trade-goods had been brought ashore, and as it yielded up its treasures the Indians gasped in amazement. Bright-colored glass beads, mirrors, red stocking caps brought forth cries of delight. Tiny metal hawkbells particularly intrigued them; their eyes sparkled with pleasure at the melodious tinkle.

One savage, bolder than his fellows, fingered the cloth of the Admiral's sleeve to feel its texture. This action gave Columbus an opportunity to fling a bright necklace around the Indian's neck. After that, the store of trade-goods diminished rapidly as one eager savage after another presented himself to be decked in similar fashion. The ice was broken. A thousand human magpies danced and chattered on the beach while as many more peered forth from the shelter of the trees.

Throughout the remainder of that fateful day, Columbus and his men remained ashore. They sampled unknown and luscious fruits, brought to them by the friendly Indians; they munched cakes of the native *cassava* bread; they bathed in the clear streams that threaded this island whose Indian name, they discovered, was Guanahani.

In token of good will the savages offered to the strangers all that they possessed: their spears, their food, and skeins of native cotton yarn, whose value the Admiral was quick to perceive. To the delight of the Spanish sailors they offered, too, tamed parrots that were able to mimic the sounds of human speech.

But it was the gold nose-pins that particularly intrigued the Admiral. By sign language he sought to discover whence the metal came. By similar means the Indians conveyed that it could be found on a large island far away to the south, called Samoet.

"That must be Cipango!" cried Martin Pinzon, his eyes ablaze. "There's no reason for us to dally here, Don Admiral, when a rich harvest awaits us elsewhere. These savages are poverty-stricken. All their miserable nose-pins wouldn't add up to the value of a thousand *maravedis*. Let us seek this Samoet at once."

When the Admiral insisted on remaining one more day at San Salvador, to make a survey of the island, Martin Alonzo showed his annoyance.

Meanwhile, the water casks were refilled. A supply of firewood was cut and taken aboard the ships. Fresh fruits, dried fish, cakes of *cassava* were stowed against future need.

Columbus invited seven of the Indians to sail with him, hoping that they might learn to speak Spanish and so become interpreters at other islands. Eagerly the invitation was accepted. It was Alfredo who at once undertook their education. Pointing to various objects—the canoes, weapons, birds, the sea—Alfredo named them in Castilian while the Indians, quick to comprehend, repeated the sound parrot-fashion. They proved to be apt and intelligent pupils.

It seemed that the glistening foliage of San Salvador had scarely dropped astern when island after island came into view, floating like shining bubbles on the sea. The seven Indians insisted that these landfalls were as numerous

as the hairs of a man's head. They had names
for more than a hundred of them.

About five leagues distant, one island larger
than the others loomed on the horizon, and here
the ships cast anchor. Columbus went ashore.
What took place he wrote that night in his
Journal in the following words:

I have christened this large island Santa Maria
de la Concepcion. I went ashore to find out if
there were any gold, for my Indians assured
me that the people wear heavy gold bracelets
on arms and legs. This was certainly only a
stratagem, for already my interpreters repent
of their bargain; they hoped to be able to
make their escape.

A canoe lay alongside the *Niña* and one of the
Indians leaped into the sea, clambered into
the canoe and paddled so quickly away that
none of my men could overtake him. Then all
the aborigines fled in every direction, like
frightened chickens.

The abandoned canoe was brought back to
the *Niña*. Another, with only one occupant,

approached the ship. This fellow was unwilling to come aboard, but he offered cotton yarn for barter. Some of the sailors leaped into the water and seized him. I had the man brought to me at once. Hanging some glass beads round his neck, and two hawkbells on his ears, I sent him home again. He wanted to present me with his yarn but I did not take it. As we were sailing away I could see the savages crowded round him on the beach.

My Indians assure me that there is a larger island to the south, which they call Colba, or Cuba. If true, it is undoubtedly Cipango. I took the altitude last night with the quadrant and found that we are 21 degrees above the equinoctial line. My calculations show that we have sailed 1,142 leagues since leaving Ferro. Surely Cuba is the mainland I seek. I shall hand over Your Majesties' letters and presents to the Grand Khan, and return at once to Spain with his reply.

But when, a day or two later, Columbus sailed into anchorage off the coast of Cuba, and the boats were sent ashore, no Grand Khan was to be found. In fact, all the inhabitants had fled their hearthfires. The villages were deserted. Fishing gear, hastily abandoned, lay about everywhere; also food, half devoured. There were even tame birds and dogs—strange mute dogs, unable to bark. But there were no people. There was no sign of gold.

When the sailors had filled their casks with water and were returning to the ship, one lone savage appeared on the edge of the jungle. Half crouched, he seemed poised for flight. Perhaps he had been sent to scout for his tribe, for he was still there when the Admiral, with an interpreter, hurried ashore. As soon as the savage was within calling distance the interpreter shouted that there was nothing to fear from the white men, that they came as friends, bearing many gifts.

On hearing the friendly declaration, scores of other Indians emerged from their hiding places. The interpreter leaped overboard and swam ashore. He was instantly surrounded by a jabbering mob. He must soon have convinced them that the Spaniards meant no harm, for a fleet of canoes put out presently to the ships. The savages chattered like sea-fowl, offering to barter their cotton for any trinkets, however cheap; but the Admiral would accept only gold. One native wore a piece of silver thrust through a hole in his ear; there was no other sign of metal. Gold was nonexistent.

Through the interpreter the Spaniards were given to understand that a powerful king lived at a distance of four days' journey. Already this potentate had been advised of the white men's arrival. Soon, the savages said—or it was thought that they did—hundreds of merchants would arrive from the capital city to barter their goods. To Christopher Columbus this could mean but one thing: at last he had reached the threshold of Cathay.

Martin Alonzo was of the same opinion. Hourly Pinzon was becoming more impatient. When, he demanded angrily, could they expect to be properly rewarded? Where were the jeweled cities of Cathay, the elephants, with gilded tusks, the streets paved with gold?

"It is clear to me," he informed his commander, "that Cuba is the mainland we have

been seeking. You can tell that by the panic of the natives. Obviously the Grand Khan comes here on slave-raids. Enough of this waiting on the pleasure of savages, I say! Give me half a dozen armed men, Don Admiral, and I shall go inland to seek the Khan himself."

Columbus agreed. Upon reaching the royal court, Pinzon was to inform the Grand Khan that the Spanish Sovereigns had sent their Admiral to these shores with letters and rich presents. The Admiral sought audience with His Highness in order to deliver these gifts.

Martin Alonzo picked his own men for the journey, among them Luis de Torres, whose knowledge of Latin, Hebrew, Chaldaic and other tongues was held to be useful in talking with the Khan. The party was to return within six days, bringing the potentate's answer, during which time the ships could be overhauled and made ready for the homeward journey.

Punctually, on the sixth of November, the weary and disheartened ambassadors returned. After a journey of some fifty miles through the inland jungle, they had come upon a large village. They were warmly welcomed. Luis de

Torres' knowledge of tongues, however, proved to be useless. The savages couldn't understand a word he said in any language. But when the native king was discovered, there was no need to question him about gold or pearls: like his subjects he was naked and very poor. He had never heard of Cipango. He had never heard of the Grand Khan. The capital city, far from being roofed with gold and studded with jewels, was a huddle of squalid huts.

One unusual fact had been discovered: the Indians had a curious habit of placing in their mouths a roll of dried leaves, which they ignited, puffing at the smoke. They called these leaves *tobaccas*. Because he did not wish to return to his commander utterly empty-handed, Martin Pinzon brought with him a supply of *tobaccas* which the Admiral promptly added to his store of curiosities. Also, the Indian chieftain had spoken of a large island to the south, called Bohio. It was certain death to go there! For Bohio was peopled by a race called *Caniba*—eaters-of-men. But Columbus scoffed at such a notion, immediately connecting the word *Caniba* with the Grand Khan.

Accordingly, orders were given to weigh anchor. The fleet, the commander informed his officers, would work forward on a southwesterly tack toward the mysterious Bohio.

Unfortunately for the plan, two of the Guanahani Indians quartered on the *Pinta* had inflamed Martin Alonzo's imagination with tales of a gold-island called Babeque, which lay to the east. Pinzon's greed had been whetted to such a degree that he completely lost his head. He brooded over the numerous differences of opinion that had marred his friendship with the Admiral. Always he had allowed Columbus's judgment to override his own. Would this enterprise, he demanded of himself, have been undertaken at all without his help? No, a thousand times! Columbus was in debt to him for every last favor. As for treating these natives with consideration—what nonsense! Let the savages bring out their gold or feel a touch of the whip!

And now this latest whimsy—to sail southwest in search of Bohio. Ridiculous! He, Martin Pinzon, would take matters into his own hands. The gold-island of Babeque lay to the east: he would sail there at once, load his ship with precious metal and be the first to return to Spain. Then let the "Don Admiral" salvage what honors he could!

Consequently, the day after quitting Cuba, the *Pinta* rapidly outdistanced the squadron. By sunset she had vanished on the horizon. Throughout an anxious night the Admiral sent up light-signals. But the signals were unanswered. On the following morning the horizon was still bare of sail. There was no longer any possibility of doubt: the *Pinta* had deserted.

Now the Admiral's fleet numbered only two ships. Should one be wrecked, there was no imagining what would happen to the expedition. To attempt to pursue the deserter was hopeless, for the *Pinta* was the fastest sailer. Columbus's heart was heavy within him, not alone for the safety of his men, but for the treacherous blow dealt by one whom he had considered a friend.

Within two days the *Santa Maria* and the *Niña* had come to the end of the Cuban coast. The commander now was forced to a decision. Unless the *Pinta* returned to the fleet, it would be unsafe to seek further for the Grand Khan

—the whole purpose of the expedition. At the moment, with a high and strange island coming into sight, the Admiral made straight for it. He could not have guessed how momentous that decision was to be.

The island was lofty and forbidding, its green heights shadowed with mystery. It seemed to terrify the Indian interpreters. They declared its name to be Haiti, its people blood-thirsty *Caniba*. They implored the Admiral to pass it by. But with a storm in the offing, Columbus had no choice but to sail into harbor. The *Santa Maria's* guns were trained to bear against possible attack. The *Niña* clung close to the protection of the larger ship. Haiti or no, the Admiral at once christened the mighty island *Hispaniola*, claiming it in the name of his sovereigns.

Canoes put rapidly out from shore. Fearfully the Spaniards eyed their approach. But the native chieftain who clambered aboard with a small army of followers was unarmed, naked and friendly. There was about him, however, a certain guile, a wariness that aroused Columbus's suspicion. He announced himself as Guacanagari the *cacique,* or king, of the island.

The Admiral stood to receive Guacanagari with all honor due his high rank. Through the interpreter, the *cacique* was informed that Columbus came as ambassador from the supreme ruler of another land, Castile: a ruler who was the most powerful prince in the whole world. But the Indian king did not believe a word of it; he was convinced that the white strangers had come straight from the sky in their great bird-like boats.

Producing some articles of gold, Columbus sought to discover if Guacanagari knew the coveted metal. With blank eyes the king stared at the gold, then shook his head. He knew nothing of gold. He pointed invitingly ashore to his village. It was modest in the extreme though surrounded by rich, green fields. The Haitians wore as little clothing as babes new-born, but it could be seen that they lived in peace and plenty.

At this point Guacanagari's manner underwent a change. Bursting into voluble speech, he pointed wildly from the gold objects in the Admiral's hand toward some place on the western horizon. He was explaining, so the interpreters declared, that in a region called Cibao gold was so plentiful that it roofed the very houses! Columbus's heart leaped with hope. Cibao! Surely this could be none other than the Indian name for Cipango! No further time should be wasted on these poverty-stricken natives. He would leave Hispaniola at once, this very evening. He forthwith sent the king ashore— the happy possessor of a pair of red shoes and a jar of orange water—and gave orders to weigh anchor.

The threat of storm had passed. A favorable land breeze was sweeping seaward and the Admiral proposed to enjoy its advantage. All his thoughts and hopes were centered on reaching Cibao as quickly as possible. Conditions were ideal for immediate departure: the inner harbor was as smooth as a lake and in the west a crescent moon glimmered.

But once again the bad fortune which had plagued Christopher Columbus for so many years made ready to strike. It was midnight on Christmas Eve when the two ships stood bravely out to the open sea. Rounding the cape which formed the eastern limit of the harbor, the wind slackened until the vessels barely made steerageway. But the coast was clear and there was no cause for alarm.

It was here that the constant watchfulness that had been forced upon Columbus by the unfriendliness of his men at last took its toll: he had been without unbroken sleep for weeks. Now he became so tired that he was unable to command the quarterdeck without an hour's rest. The pilot Cosa knew his business and it was the chief officer's watch. Surely they were capable of looking after the ship for an hour! Giving them his final instructions, Columbus staggered below to his cabin. Fully clothed, he fell across his bunk and was instantly asleep.

Not often had Cosa enjoyed such relief from watchfulness. He, too, was weary and saw no reason why he should stay awake while that foreign-born "Admiral"—rot his bones!—lost himself in dreams. Cosa beckoned to one of the ship's boys; he gave him the helm and in a low voice instructed him how to hold the course. The officer of the watch, dozing in the moon-cast shadow of the mainsail, noticed nothing. Then Cosa crept to his cabin. In such fashion had Martin Pinzon's desertion undermined the authority of the commander-in-chief.

No ship's boy had ever been trusted with the *Santa Maria's* helm. The tide was on the ebb and a strong current was urging the flagship toward a hidden sandbar that jutted far out from the cape. But the boy at the helm, holding the course as instructed, noticed nothing amiss. So gently did the caravel strike the sandbar, and lodge herself there, that no perceptible shock was felt. Not until the rudder refused to respond did the unfortunate boy realize what had happened. Then, in a panic, he shouted for Cosa. That individual not responding, the boy began to blubber as he fought the jammed helm.

The officer of the watch awoke. A great oath burst from his lips. "*Santissima!* You've run us aground! We're sinking!"

He seized the cord of the ship's bell and clanged it violently: a signal reserved only for extreme peril. Instantly the whole ship was in uproar. Men poured up from below like rats deserting a doomed vessel. The clamor of the bell threw everyone into terror.

Aroused by the noise, Columbus bounded up

the companionway. He did not need the roar of the breakers, so close at hand, to tell him what had happened. He felt rather than heard the rasp of his ship's keel as she drove deeper and deeper into the sand. Already she listed badly to starboard. Foothold was difficult on the canting deck. Ashore in a savage country! God help them all!

"Lower away the longboat!" shouted the commander. "Jump to it, men! Cast the anchor astern. We may be able to warp her off——"

Frantically the boat was lowered from the davits. The chief officer and half a dozen men leaped aboard, seized the oars. But instead of obeying their captain's command, they rowed off into the darkness, in the direction of the *Nina,* thinking thus to make themselves safe aboard the other ship. The Admiral and the rest of the crew could go to the bottom for all they cared!

Desertion of his post in face of peril was the most serious crime a sailor could commit—a crime punishable by death. But bitterly Columbus knew that he would be unable to punish the miserable wretches who had abandoned him:

the spirit of rebellion that Martin Pinzon had loosed was ripe for mutiny.

Deserted by a part of his crew, with the tide ebbing and his ship at a perilous cant, he took the desperate remedy of cutting away the mainmast. But every effort was useless. The panic-stricken crew had no thought but for themselves. Already the cover of the main hatch had burst open; when the tide turned, the *Santa Maria* would, literally, drown. With set jaw the Admiral hurried below. He gathered up his charts, his Journal, his few instruments. Then, after the last of his men had been rowed to safety aboard the *Niña*, he abandoned his ship to her fate. Now the little *Niña* alone remained to carry a hundred men back across the wide ocean.

Dawn revealed the flagship still lodged on her final resting place. But she had not yet broken up. Swarms of Indians in canoes helped to bring the cargo ashore. A shelter of palm-leaf thatch was hastily contrived. King Guacanagari himself supervised the operation. And so eager were the Indians to help, so hard and honestly

did they work, that the entire cargo was sal-
vaged without the loss of a single object. This
prompt and generous assistance made a profound impression on the Admiral, and greatly
influenced his future course.

The shipwreck had one immediate and far-
reaching result: in being forced to go ashore to
Guacanagari's village, Columbus saw for the first
time the Indian women. He was astounded to
discover that they wore heavy bracelets of yellow metal around arms and ankles. *Gold!* Some
had curiously wrought necklaces, others elabor-
ate nose-pins. This discovery threw the whole
ship's company into wildest excitement. Here at
last were the promised treasures of Cathay!

Confronted by the truth, Guacanagari acted
like a child caught out in a lie. He pretended to
have misunderstood Columbus's question about
the gold. Confessing to much more of the
precious metal in hiding, he promised to trade it
for the Spaniards' trinkets. There were, he said,
rich mines high in the mountains, filled with
more gold than all the ships in the world could
carry away.

Where the Admiral had despaired at the loss

of the *Santa Maria*, it now seemed as if his bad luck had been turned into a stroke of marvelous fortune. True, his ship would leave her bones on the sands of Hispaniola; but here was a land of wealth unimaginable, to find which he had dreamed all his life.

The following morning, after divine service, Christopher Columbus informed his men that he had decided to found the first Spanish settlement in the New World.

"It must be clear to all of you," he explained, "that it is impossible for the *Niña* to carry the crews of two ships. I call for volunteers to build a fort! Supplies will be left here—enough to last a year. I shall carry the good tidings of our discovery to Their Majesties, then return with a large fleet to take you home. Who will be the first to volunteer?"

So many hands were raised that it was difficult to choose among the men. At last some thirty-nine of them were picked: a hardy breed, fired by a love of adventure and a greed for gold. Or perhaps, recalling the toil and hardship which would be their lot if they returned to Europe, the men saw the simple life of the savages in

rosiest hue. Among them the Admiral chose a
cooper, a carpenter, a physician, a tailor, a
caulker, and a master-gunner to serve the falconets. He appointed Diego de Aranda as commander-in-chief.

The duty of this group would be to collect
gold and spices, to discover the mines and for-
ests which produced these treasures, so that a
vast store would be ready against the Admiral's
return.

The work of building the fort began at once.
All hands fell to chopping down trees: the air
rang to a clamor of axe and adze. The willing
Indians toiled like slaves.

In less than a week a large blockhouse had
been constructed. It was surrounded by a pro-
tecting barricade of stout saplings lashed together. The *Santa Maria* was stripped of furn-
ishings to render the blockhouse comfortable.
The ship's arquebuses and falconets thrust their
muzzles through openings in the roof. Hogs-
heads of salted meat, dried fish, bacon, lard, oil
and wine were stored under lock and key. The
settlement was christened La Navidad—the Na-
tivity—in honor of the day on which Columbus

had made his disastrous landing on this wild shore.

By the second day of January, 1493, the Admiral felt that he could safely leave the little company behind. He was haunted by the fear that Martin Pinzon might be the first to reach Spain, and not only claim the glory and rewards of discovery, but destroy the reputation and character of the leader.

Columbus firmly believed Hispaniola to be the island of Cipango (Japan) just beyond which lay the fabulous country of the Grand Khan. The amazing store of gold which Guacanagari had traded for trinkets was convincing proof of this. Even if the palaces with golden roofs, the elephants with gilded tusks, the pearls and rubies of Marco Polo had not yet been discovered, he was convinced that he stood on the very threshold of their possession. He would return to Spain, then come back to Hispaniola with a fleet of twenty ships. Gold would shower upon his Sovereigns, fulfilling the most extravagant promise!

As added insurance for the safety of the men who would be left behind, it was necessary to impress Guacanagari with a display of power. Since the Indians had never heard a gun fired, the Admiral ordered several shots aimed at the hulk of the *Santa Maria* from the fort's guns.

At the first belch of flame and thunder, the Indians fell flat to the ground, as if struck by lightning. They beheld the ship's great timbers flung up into the air like straws in the wind. Another miracle of the white man! Then the Spaniards formed ranks on the beach and indulged in a sham battle with crossbows and muskets. That left the Indians silent with fear.

Now, for the last time, Columbus faced his men. His voice was grave as he gave them his final charge: "You must remember that these Indians, savage though they seem, are subjects of the Spanish Crown, even as you yourselves. You are to treat them with all kindness. Obey your commander, who serves in my stead. I take leave of you in pride of the honorable mission that every one of you has to fulfill. Your names shall be writ in glory! God's blessing on you all."

The longboat lay waiting at the water's edge. The *Niña* tugged at her hawser. Guacanagari pressed Columbus to his breast, rubbing his nose against the Admiral's cheek, after the manner of his people's leave-taking. The dense throng of Indians on the beach broke into noisy wailing. The thirty-nine men who would stay at La Navidad wore solemn faces. They who had been so eager to remain, thought now about their homeland, of the long months of waiting that must pass before they saw their loved ones again, or heard the laughter of their children. In that moment how could they have guessed that when, true to his word, the Admiral returned to Hispaniola ten months later, he would find only the ashes of the stockade, some mutilated bodies, a huddle of tattered clothing to mark the site of La Navidad . . .

The sailors bent to the oars. The longboat swept across the harbor, past the bleaching skeleton of the *Santa Maria,* out toward the ship waiting expectantly at anchor. Standing in the sternsheets, Christopher Columbus waved his last farewell—to his men, to the New World.

CHAPTER 9

The Last Long Journey

RAIN DRIPPED HEAVILY FROM THE EAVES OF
the houses, ran in streams through the cobbled
streets of Valladolid. Under a leaden sky all
Spain seemed to hold its breath with waiting.

Within the Franciscan cloister, in a poorly
furnished chamber, a young man fanned the
glow of a charcoal fire to rob the room of its

chill. Beside the fire, a tall, gaunt figure sat motionless, his eyes closed.

The young man's heart twisted; fifteen years had passed since he, then a boy of eight, had climbed the hills of Palos with his father to seek shelter at La Rabida. During those years, much had happened to the man who sat beside the fire, now ill, broken, grown old before his time. And Diego wanted to cry out against the monstrous injustice which had brought this man, like some splendid eagle, to earth. How wasted was the once-powerful frame of Christopher Columbus! Only the eyes remained unchanged, vital and restless and alive.

"My son——" Columbus murmured.

"Yes, *padrecito*," Diego replied. "What is your wish?"

"The letter—you have written it?"

"I am beginning now, my father."

"Make haste . . . I should like to know that it has been delivered before——" The voice faltered.

"Before what, *padrecito?*"

A corner of the Admiral's thin lips quirked. "Before I set sail—once again . . ."

As in a dream Diego stood looking down at the wasted figure, so still, so faintly smiling. Of what was Christopher Columbus thinking? Was he remembering, perhaps, as the aged do, scenes of long ago: the sunlit strand of Genoa; the magical isles of the Indies; the empty sound of men's acclaim; the false glitter of gold . . . ?

Heavily, as one who has no heart in such a task, Diego seated himself at a table by the window, reached for a quill. The parchment blurred across his sight as he wrote:—

May 20, 1506— Valladolid, Spain
To Father Juan Perez, Prior of
Our Lady of La Rabida

Reverend Sir:—It has long grieved my father that the fortunes of his latter years have prevented him from grasping your hand. For it is you he counts as the one friend most often tried and unfailingly true. He asks me to give you the facts of what has befallen him, since his enemies are many and their lies have warped the truth.

I fear that the longest journey of all lies before him, and he is but waiting the summons to set sail. I know not what his illness may be, but in his heart he bleeds to death. His life rose in poverty, reached a zenith of earthly glory, and now sets in eclipse. King Ferdinand does not see fit to fulfill that which he promised by word and seal; and our Lady Queen—my father's one true friend at Court—lies dead.

The Admiral has become what he was in the beginning: a voice in the wilderness, a troublesome beggar at the door of kings. But I anticipate . . .

You will recall that fateful spring of 1493, when word of Hispaniola's existence was first brought back to astound the world. Undoubtedly you have heard of Martin Pinzon's desertion, of how he made his way back to Spain and sent word to Their Majesties that the discoveries of a New World were his own. By God's grace, the Admiral himself had reached Granada but a day or two before, and apprised our sovereigns of the truth. Pinzon died shortly thereafter, in bitterness and shame.

Never was a man more highly honored than my father! He was cheered, blessed, acclaimed for his great discovery. I rode at his side to Barcelona, where the Court was, through happy crowds that tossed flowers to us as we passed. What a procession! A train of mules carried the exhibits brought from the New World: cages full of birds of brilliant plumage, the like of which had never been seen. I remember the cage of *iguanas*—giant lizards that drew gasps of horror from all beholders.

And the troop of Indians—only six of them left alive—but striding through the streets with the grace of animals. Some had painted their faces; they brandished javelins and bows. All wore the feathered headdresses of their people, and golden ornaments. Parrots perched on their wrists like falcons.

Then came the seamen and mariners—the same men who had fought and roistered and mutinied at Hispaniola—but who now were playful as puppies on their home heath. After them followed the Admiral himself, splendidly mounted. Erect in the saddle, in doublet of crimson laced with gold, he was a regal figure— a Don in all truth. And at his side rode the proudest boy in Christendom—a boy garbed in cloth-of-silver and a plumed cap, as befitted the page of a princeling.

It was already the middle of April and the air was like the wine of Malaga. The royal throne had been set up under a silken pavilion, and in the hot sunshine of that glorious day, Their Majesties awaited the coming of the great man. The entire Court was in attendance: nobles and their ladies, knights of Santiago and Calatrava; the Cardinal of Spain in scarlet from head to toe; and my father's old enemy, Hernando de Talavera.

To a flourish of trumpets the Admiral dismounted, tossed the reins to a groom. Tall, commanding, his head held high, he stood arrested for a second, the focus of every eye. He savoured this hour of triumph. Here was a moment of supreme significance in the history of the world, and he knew it.

Then in a gesture without precedent the King and Queen rose from their chairs-of-state to receive the honored guest. The oldest courtier could not remember such an astounding compliment! It hastened the Admiral's step. He knelt to kiss the hands extended in such kindly wel-

come. The Queen herself raised him from his
knees.

"You shall sit beside us, Don Admiral," she
said, smiling. "And tell us of your great adventure."

Her words broke the ice in Christopher Columbus's heart, set springs to flowing.

"May it please Your Highness," he cried, "before I speak of an empire whose wealth is still
unguessed, let me assure you that I do not return with empty hands. The treasures that I lay
at your feet are but specimens, tokens of the vast
store which waits only for ships to bring them
back to Spain."

He summoned his train of bearers with their
samples of booty. They carried gold in dust, in
nuggets and lumps; barbaric masks with golden
ornamentation; baskets of gums and spices and
bales of raw cotton; timbers of unknown wood.
And lastly the proud golden-skinned Indians
themselves, who bowed their foreheads on the
carpet in obeisance to their new Sovereigns.

As the savages rose and moved to one side of
the dais, an Indian youth advanced, naked save
for a waist-cloth. Upon one wrist he carried a

parrot of brilliant plumage. Moving toward the throne, the youth knelt with the lithe grace of a cat. He placed his head close to the parrot's, coaxed it with a murmur. The bird cocked its bright eyes, then opened its beak in clear though raucous speech.

"Long life to Ferdinand the King!" it screeched. "Long life to gracious Isabella!"

A gasp went through the assemblage. A bird with the power of human speech! None had ever heard the like. The Indian boy flashed a grin of triumph as once again the bird spoke:

"Long life to Don Christopher Columbus, Admiral of the Ocean Seas!"

"By Saint James!" exclaimed the King. "What miracles are these?"

"They are but trifles, Highness," the Admiral assured his sovereign. "I bring you dominion over a realm larger than the whole kingdom of Spain! Millions of human beings, whose existence no one suspected, are now your subjects. Their conversion to Christianity will reward Your Majesties with temporal and eternal grace."

"You have triumphed beyond our fondest hope, O Columbus," cried the Queen. "How happy the day I pledged my necklace to your aid!"

"I have been permitted to do what no other mortal man has dared," the other returned. "Highness, let sacred festivals be held! Let churches be decorated with green boughs and flowers, so that God in Heaven may rejoice over the earth, and over the spread of His Kingdom among heathen nations!"

The words rang out into the hushed quiet. When Columbus had finished speaking he bowed his white head and sank to his knees. The King and Queen knelt beside him, while the voices of the Choir Royal burst into a triumphant *Almighty God, we praise Thee.*

Christopher Columbus was the hero of the hour. Men forgot for the moment what they had formerly remembered, and were to remember again: that the Admiral was a foreigner of lowly birth. Now they saw him as the spearhead of empire, the emblem of power and riches. Alas, how short a time he was to bask in the fickle sunshine of their favor!

Only Hernando de Talavera withheld his praise.

"Had you never made your voyage, Don Christopher," the Archbishop purred, "surely in this our Spain, where there has never been a lack of daring mariners, there would have been another who made bold to do what you have done."

Columbus smiled straight into the eyes of his old foe. He dispatched a page to fetch an egg. Then he spun the egg on a table and said: "I wager a thousand gold florins, Your Eminence, that neither you nor any other can do with this egg what I shall do with it: namely, make it stand upright without falling!"

From hand to hand the egg was passed around the assemblage; but none, including de Talavera, could make it stand. When it returned to the Admiral, he cracked the shell at one end, forming a flat surface upon which the egg stood readily enough.

"You see, my lord Archbishop," Columbus murmured, "that once a man has ventured to do a thing, it afterwards seems easy enough for another to accomplish!"

During the next weeks, the Admiral was much in the company of his Sovereigns, the object of their flattering attention. They caused a coat-of-arms to be made for him, in which the lion of Aragon and the castle of Castile were quartered with a device of his own choosing. All his demands were met. Not only was he a Don, a Viceroy and Governor of all the islands of his discovery, he was now Captain-General of a fleet of seventeen vessels and three transports. An army of fifteen hundred men—sailors, soldiers, miners, artisans, all who seemed necessary to the founding of a colony—was assembled under his command.

When he left Barcelona at the end of May, escorted by the whole Court, Christopher Columbus was one of the most powerful men in Spain. But now he no longer shouldered the whole responsibility: he was to share it with Fonseca, the newly appointed head of the Colonial Office. Once the machinery of government was in working order, the function of an admiral became the making of new discoveries. How soon after that would come the moment when he could be dispensed with!

And how different from the first voyage was this second! Where men had been bribed or bludgeoned into the Admiral's service, now there were more offers than could be accepted. The Sea of Darkness had lost its terrors. Beyond its western boundaries lay a land where golden nuggets were as common as pebbles. In place of the three original ships, the stately caravels were the finest of the Spanish fleet. Columbus's older brother, Bartolomeo, whom he had not seen in many years, came from Genoa to join the expedition.

In high expectation the fleet set sail. At Gomera, in the Canaries, a most important cargo was taken aboard: cattle, sheep, goats, pigs; mastiffs for watchdogs; horses, mules and donkeys. The next port of call would be La Navidad, Hispaniola.

As early as the fifth of November, the Sea of Darkness had been safely crossed and a new island rose on the horizon. Columbus christened it Dominica, "Lord's Day," because it was sighted in the early twilight of a Sunday morning. It was here that the first bananas were discovered, and the Spaniards found them good. It was here, also, that they had their first encounter with the dreaded *Caribs*—the ill-famed cannibals about whom the Guanahani Indians had spoken in whispers.

At first sight their villages seemed deserted; but the Admiral's men were too uncomfortably aware that they were being watched from ambush. Clusters of human skulls hung from the door posts of the houses. And as the sailors hunted through the abandoned dwellings, they came upon a sight to chill the stoutest heart: gnawed bones and portions of human limbs roasting on spits over the embers.

It was with a vast sense of relief that the Admiral gave the order to up-anchor. A course was laid immediately for Hispaniola.

Two days later the eastern tip of that island came into view. The stately fleet swung to anchor off the site of the first settlement in the New World. The ships were too large, however, to enter the bay.

It seemed strange that where, but ten months before, the beach had swarmed with savages, there was now no sight or sound of human beings. None of the men from the fort could be seen. At the Admiral's order two cannon shots

were fired. No answer returned. An ominous silence hung like a shroud over the green land. Why did not the garrison return the salute? A sense of premonition, like a chill, passed over all hands.

In that moment the Admiral *knew* what had happened, but he took pains to conceal his fears from the men. When at last a single canoe put out from the shore, it carried only five timid Indians. Coming aboard, they informed the Admiral that their king, Guacanagari, had been wounded by enemies—the owners of the gold mines. The Indians also announced that the entire garrison of the Spanish fort had been wiped out. The settlement was but a charred relic.

And what a difference in the attitude of the Indians themselves! Their friendliness and generosity gone, they slunk sullenly out of sight. When Columbus was rowed ashore to seek out the king, he was sickened by a glimpse of the blackened ruins of the fort. What had come to pass after his departure from Hispaniola he could only imagine, but Guacanagari confirmed his worst suspicions. The Indian king, who had indeed been wounded, was found lying in an improvised hut, surrounded by a handful of retainers.

The chieftain wept bitterly as he pressed the Admiral's hand. In broken voice he said: "Greed and jealousy destroyed your men, Don Admiral. Their brutal treatment turned my people into enemies. Your men sought gold in Caonabo's province. All were slain. Those at the fort quarreled among themselves. There were none to defend La Navidad against Caonabo when he came."

With heavy heart Christopher Columbus chose the site for a second settlement. He was determined that his men should have no leisure to ponder the tragic fate of their brothers. Work began in earnest. The livestock was unloaded and pens were built. Trees were felled. A church was laid out. Wheat, corn, oats were planted. Shoots of olive, lemon and orange trees, carefully nurtured during the long voyage, were set out.

Indeed, all work progressed so vigorously that by the seventh of February the church was completed; it was consecrated with solemn ceremony.

From a scaffold beside the nave a bronze bell pealed forth into the jungle—a sound that seemed to enrapture the Indians who remained near the Spanish settlement. At night, even the untamed Caonabo and his warriors crept down from the hills to listen, spellbound, to the magical voice. That bell was to play a role of its own . . .

In the nearby river, miners discovered abundant signs of gold whose sources were certainly high up in Caonabo's domain. Torn between greed and the fear of the savage tribe which had slain their fellows, the Spaniards rebelled against the irksome labor of building this settlement called Isabella. They had not come out to the New World to toil like slaves in the sun. Even if it called for the whip, let the Indians themselves be put to such degrading tasks, not them! Grimly Columbus overheard the mutters; he knew that a day of reckoning approached.

But the Indians, lured to the settlement by promises of beads and hawkbells, no longer were so humbly obedient in the presence of the "sons of heaven." The least imaginative of the men understood that warfare lurked in the background. The Admiral's haste to fortify the settlement was proof enough!

At this point, the Admiral dispatched twelve caravels back to Spain for fresh supplies, sending with them a score of Indians who were to be trained as interpreters and converted to Christianity. Columbus was impatient to get on with his explorations. The kingdom of the Grand Khan had still to be discovered!

Despite the sense of hostility in the air, he persuaded himself that Isabella was now securely enough fortified against attack so that he could leave Pedro Margarite, one of his ablest lieutenants, in command. Margarite was cautioned above all else to pacify the Indians. On the twenty-fourth of April the Admiral sailed westward with three caravels.

Through island after island in the Lesser Antilles the little fleet picked its way. But the kingdom of the Khan was not to be found. The only reward was the discovery of maize. Seeds of this Indian grain were at once collected for transport to Europe. It was on this trip, too, that Columbus was first stricken with the fever that was to plague him to the last of his days and hasten his end. For the rest, the uncertain temper and the exhaustion of his crew compelled the Admiral at last to abandon his search. Reluctantly he returned to Hispaniola.

During his short absence, he found that the Indians everywhere had risen in arms. Instead of pacifying them, Pedro Margarite's actions had transformed them into deadly foes. To cap this disaster, rather than face his commander-in-chief, Margarite had seized a caravel and decamped to Spain. There, before the King and Queen, the entire blame for the state of affairs in Hispaniola would be placed upon the Admiral's shoulders. This was the situation that greeted a man half-dead and sore beset.

Immediately Columbus appointed his brother Bartolomeo, a most excellent man, Governor of Isabella. He had but one other subordinate whom he felt that he could trust: a young noble named Alonzo de Hojeda. Realizing that no peace could exist between Spaniard and Indian until King Caonabo had been captured, Columbus despatched Hojeda into the mountains for that brave purpose.

Whatever flaws of character Alonzo de Hojeda subsequently revealed, cowardice was not one of them. In the Moorish wars he had pitted his skill against hardier foes than untrained Indians. He knew all the subterfuges of warfare. With only ten men at his command, he set out boldly for the mountain fortress where Caonabo had assembled thousands of warriors. After a journey of some three days, the Spaniards rode confidently into the very stronghold of the savage king. In fact, so daring was Hojeda's bluff that Caonabo and his *caciques* were dumfounded by the maneuver. The fact that the Spaniards moved among them as if they were invited guests must mean, the Indians felt, that they possessed great hidden powers . . . Hojeda played his cards well. The Admiral, he declared, understood that Caonabo was the mightiest chieftain in Hispaniola. To attain his friendship and establish peace, Columbus offered the most valuable gift in the world: the bronze church bell of Isabella!

Caonabo's eyes glistened. The church bell! For his very own! He could hang it from the rafters of his dwelling and listen to its voice in every wind. His decision was made at once.

"In return for the speaking bell," he said slowly, "I pledge my friendship to the men of Spain. Let there be peace between us!"

"You have chosen wisely, O king," Hojeda replied smoothly. "But the bell is of great weight. There are not enough men in all Isabella to carry it up into these mountains. Caonabo himself must bring men to fetch the bell if he wants it."

"We shall start at once," the King declared.

It was a strange procession that filed slowly out of the Indian stronghold: Alonzo de Hojeda and his ten men well mounted on fast horses, five thousand barefoot warriors at their backs. Caonabo himself strode proudly beside Hojeda's horse, his place beside the Spanish chieftain. From the cantle of Hojeda's saddle dangled a chain of gleaming silver with handcuffs attached. What, Caonabo demanded, was the purpose of the chain? Informed that it was a magic charm, direct from heaven, the Indian understood at once: every chieftain had his own *turi*—his magic. This was the white man's *turi*.

Fascinated, Caonabo could not take his eyes from that gleaming chain. Might he, he begged, be allowed to touch it? But Hojeda was reluctant. Such *turi* was only to be touched by kings . . . Still, Caonabo was a great noble in his own land and a friend of Spain . . . Yes, he might be allowed to touch the chain, even to wear it for a moment . . .

The party had halted for noon in an open valley. Hojeda's mind was made up. It was a bold stroke by which the Spaniards must stand or fall. He himself slipped the chains around the Indian king's wrists. The manacles snapped shut.

"You shall ride with me on my horse, that all your men may see you wearing the magic *turi*," Hojeda said, smiling.

Willing hands boosted Caonabo up to the saddle. Hojeda supported him there firmly. The horsemen rode slowly through the ranks of the warriors, circling always toward the other edge. The savages were filled with awe at this mark of the white man's esteem: their chief wearing the magic *turi*. They stretched themselves out on the ground.

Then with a shout Hojeda put the spurs to his mount. The animal leaped forward into the open plain. The other horses thundered in pursuit. Wildly the Indians came to their senses, understood the trick. Their leader was being captured. Pandemonium broke loose. But no Indian could keep up with those galloping steeds. Arrows fell short. Riding like the wind, the Spaniards with their captive raced over mountain and plain, seeking the safety of Isabella.

The capture of the chief united all the tribes of Hispaniola in warfare against the invader. Thousands strong, shrieking like demons out of darkness, they stormed the little settlement. But their javelins and bows were no match for the arquebuses and muskets that spat fire and destruction in their ranks. Before the counter-attacks of Hojeda and his lancers the bravest chieftains gave way. Too, aiding the Spaniards were great dogs that pursued the naked fugitives, pulled them to the ground and tore them to pieces. It was only a question of time . . . Soon, indeed, the Spaniards would be truly masters of this unhappy land.

In the meantime, Pedro Margarite had accomplished his wicked purpose: Queen Isabella's faith was not easily shaken; but the King had been persuaded that Columbus was an incompetent. Moreover, here was an opportunity to be rid of a Viceroy whose claims always had been too extravagant . . . The King sent Governor Aguado to seize the Admiral's place.

Aghast at this reversal, Columbus at once hurried back to Spain to protest the appointment. Alas, he found the people had lost all interest in the lands across the sea. This time no honor greeted him, no triumphal parade. King Ferdinand, repudiating his promises, kept him waiting at Court for over a year before granting six ships for a third voyage and a miserable crew of five hundred jailbirds. Furthermore, the Admiral was commanded to stay away from Hispaniola.

It was on this third journey that the mainland of the American continent was discovered, in the region near the mouth of the Orinoco River. But by now, so broken in health was Columbus, so wasted by fever, that it was necessary to have his bed set up on the quarterdeck where he might direct the sailing of his ship.

Years of labor over charts, as well as the punish-
ing tropical sunlight, had left him with a mysterious malady of the eyes, so that for days at a
time he was almost without sight.

His three ships proved to be unseaworthy, his
ragtag crew were quickly out of hand. In dire
straits, the Admiral once more was forced to
seek the shelter of Hispaniola, though he had
been forbidden to do so.

August of 1498 found the settlement seething
with rebellion. Governor Aguado had been mur-
dered. Columbus's brother Bartolomeo had
again taken command. A group of malcontents
had split the colony into two camps. Gathering
the most lawless of the men, a settler named Roldan plotted the overthrow of Columbus and his
brother. Abandoned by the crown, the Admiral
was at the caprice and insolence of Roldan and
his confederates.

Daily, matters went from bad to worse. It
was simple for Roldan to win over the Indians
with false promises, to assure them that the
Admiral had been deposed and that he, Roldan,
was now their leader.

In the midst of this turmoil a caravel arrived

from Spain, dropped anchor off Isabella. It carried the king's new emissary, one Don Francisco de Bobadilla, sent to inquire into the state of affairs at Hispaniola. At once he took hold with a high hand. Columbus and Bartolomeo both were seized, imprisoned and clapped in irons. In such shameful fashion was a great man, wildly acclaimed but a few years since, sent back home to face his sovereigns.

Columbus submitted to the disgrace without resistance: the will of the king must be obeyed! But he and Bartolomeo were not allowed to communicate with each other. Throughout the torturing voyage they lay in solitary confinement, weighted like common criminals with their irons.

News of the Admiral's shame sped like wildfire across the countryside. All Spain was horrified. Cries of indignation soon reached the royal Court at Granada. The Queen at once dispatched a message to her fallen favorite, with 2000 gold florins for clothing in keeping with his rank.

But when once again the Admiral presented himself before his sovereigns, his eyesight had so failed that he stumbled on the steps of the dais and collapsed at Isabella's feet. The good Queen's eyes filled with tears. Even haughty Ferdinand vowed that the high-handed Bobadilla should answer for his insolence. The monarchs listened sympathetically to the whole story, promising that all injustices should be righted in due time. Physicians were appointed to care for the stricken man. He was forbidden even to think of another voyage until he had regained strength and health.

But that was never to be. The sense of dedication which had always been with Christopher Columbus allowed him no peace. Though Spain, at that time beset by enemies, had no ships to spare, the Admiral at last persuaded his sovereigns that he was ready to set sail once again. This time, four miserable caravels were placed at his disposal, with a hundred and fifty ill-found men.

It was on the ninth of May, 1502, that Columbus set out from Cadiz on his fourth and last voyage. Bartolomeo accompanied him, the one happy circumstance of the undertaking, as will be seen. From the beginning it was an ill-omened enterprise. The vessels were floating rat traps, the crews little better than mutineers.

Unafraid, the Admiral set a course for Central America, where the mighty Orinoco poured its floods into the ocean. For he had heard rumors of another and vaster ocean, far to the west, where the elusive empire of the Great Khan glimmered like a mirage . . .

But violent storms, sweeping down from the Orinoco delta, drove the little fleet back and back. The ships were stripped of canvas. Their masts snapped. Their seams gaped. On the unfriendly shores of Jamaica they crept for safety. There the Indians were savage. A hail of arrows greeted the Spaniards. With greatest difficulty were the Indians driven off. Thirst and starvation faced the wrecked men. The ships were hopelessly crippled.

There was only once chance for survival: someone must paddle in a canoe across the open ocean that separated Jamaica from Hispaniola, seeking aid! Bartolomeo volunteered. It was with a heavy heart that Christopher Columbus watched his brother set out on the perilous journey. Too well he understood how slight was the chance of salvation.

Bartolomeo reached Hispaniola. But the Governor let many months elapse before he sent a ship to rescue the doomed men. When at last God in His mercy again allowed the Admiral to reach Spain, it was to discover that Isabella the Queen—his only friend—lay dead . . .

The quill dropped from Diego's numb fingers. Beside the fire, the gaunt figure in the chair stirred.

"You have finished the letter, my son——?"

"It is done, *padrecito*."

"Good lad . . . Come here, over here where I may look at you——"

Diego rose, moved over to his father's side, gripped the wasted hand in both his own. The restless eyes looked up into his, the thin lips softened with a smile. "My son, my poor boy! How much I had hoped for you. How bitterly I have failed!"

Above the tightness in his throat, Diego cried out: "*Padrecito*, never say that! As long as men live, your name will be upon their tongues. You are a great man!"

Slowly the other shook his head. "Ah, no, my

Diego. Not a great man. I have but opened a door that others might enter . . . Look, there is light in the sky! The storm is past. Soon the sun will shine for us again——"

Involuntarily Diego turned toward the window. A band of light, bright-minted as gold, had pierced the leaden sky. It slanted down to earth like a vast golden ladder leading upward to another world . . . And as the young man stood there, watching, a miracle began to happen. Soon the wonder would be lost, never to be believed . . . And he knew that behind him his father's questing spirit, as everlasting as the sky, was climbing up that golden ladder, so like the shrouds of some heroic vessel whose maintruck was a star . . .

"Padre!" whispered Diego, brokenly. "Ah, *padrecito!"*